Through *the* Bible

BOOK BY BOOK

PART

NEW TESTAMENT

MATTHEW <u>TO</u> ACTS

THREE

Myer Pearlman

MY HEALTHY CHURCH

02-7003

FOREWORD

Through the Bible Book by Book, a classic introductory guide to understanding the 66 books of the Bible, has been translated into numerous languages. It has been a standard classroom text for more than seven decades in churches and schools, as well as an aid for personal Bible study.

The author, Myer Pearlman (1898-1943), was one of the foremost theologians in the Assemblies of God in the 1930s and 1940s. Raised in an observant Jewish family in Birmingham, England, he learned the Torah (Old Testament) and Hebrew as a boy. Pearlman's family moved to the United States when he was a teenager. After serving in the U.S. Army during World War I, Pearlman returned to America and accepted Christ at a small Pentecostal mission in San Francisco.

Pearlman enrolled at the newly opened Central Bible Institute (now Central Bible College, Springfield, Missouri) in 1922. Upon graduation, the principal, Frank M. Boyd, invited Pearlman to join the faculty.

Noted for his prolific pen, Pearlman authored numerous textbooks and the early years of the Assemblies of God adult Sunday school curriculum. At a time when anti-Semitism was on the rise in Europe and in America, it is significant that the Assemblies of God entrusted a Jewish-born theologian with such a significant responsibility. Pearlman's background, however, made him a uniquely qualified biblical scholar within the Pentecostal movement.

After years of constant writing, teaching and preaching, Pearlman literally worked himself to death. Myer Pearlman died on July 16, 1943, in Springfield, Missouri.

Darrin J. Rodgers, Director
Flower Pentecostal Heritage Center

ABBREVIATIONS FOR
THE BOOKS OF THE BIBLE

Old Testament

Genesis	Gen.
Exodus	Ex.
Leviticus	Lev.
Numbers	Num.
Deuteronomy	Deut.
Joshua	Josh.
Judges	Jud.
Ruth	Ruth
1 Samuel	1 Sam.
2 Samuel	2 Sam.
1 Kings	1 Kings
2 Kings	2 Kings
1 Chronicles	1 Chron.
2 Chronicles	2 Chron.
Ezra	Ezra
Nehemiah	Neh.
Esther	Est.
Job	Job
Psalms	Ps.
Proverbs	Prov.
Ecclesiastes	Ecc.
Song of Solomon	S. of Sol.
Isaiah	Isa.
Jeremiah	Jer.
Lamentations	Lam.
Ezekiel	Ezek.
Daniel	Dan.
Hosea	Hosea
Joel	Joel
Amos	Amos
Obadiah	Oba.
Jonah	Jonah
Micah	Micah

Nahum	Nahum
Habbakuk	Hab.
Zephaniah	Zeph.
Haggai	Hag.
Zechariah	Zech.
Malachi	Mal.

New Testament

Matthew	Matt.
Mark	Mark
Luke	Luke
John	John
Acts of the Apostles	Acts
Romans	Rom.
1 Corinthians	1 Cor.
2 Corinthians	2 Cor.
Galatians	Gal.
Ephesians	Eph.
Philippians	Phil.
Colossians	Col.
1 Thessalonians	1 Thess.
2 Thessalonians	2 Thess.
1 Timothy	1 Tim.
2 Timothy	2 Tim.
Titus	Titus
Philemon	Phile.
Hebrews	Heb.
James	James
1 Peter	1 Peter
2 Peter	2 Peter
1 John	1 John
2 John	2 John
3 John	3 John
Jude	Jude
Revelation	Rev.

CHAPTER I

BOOKS OF THE NEW TESTAMENT

Learn the following classification:
  I. The Gospels, dealing with the
     manifestation of our salvation.
      1. Matthew
      2. Mark
      3. Luke
      4. John
 II. The historical book, dealing with the
     propagation of our salvation.
     1. The Acts
III. The doctrinal books, dealing with the
     explanation of our salvation.
     The Pauline Epistles
      1. Romans
      2. 1 Corinthians
      3. 2 Corinthians
      4. Galatians
      5. Ephesians
      6. Philippians
      7. Colossians
      8. 1 Thessalonians
      9. 2 Thessalonians
     10. 1 Timothy
     11. 2 Timothy
     12. Titus
     13. Philemon
     14. Hebrews
   The General Epistles
      1. James
      2. 1 Peter

   3. 2 Peter
   4. 1 John
   5. 2 John
   6. 3 John
   7. Jude
 IV. The prophetical book, dealing with the
      consummation of our salvation.
      1. Revelation

THE FOUR GOSPELS

The first question that confronts us before commencing the study of the Gospels is, Why four Gospels? Why not two, three, or just one? This can best be answered by stating the fact that, in apostolic times, there were four representative classes of people—the Jews, the Romans, the Greeks, and that body taken from all three classes, the Church. Each one of the evangelists wrote for these respective classes, and adapted himself to their character, needs, and ideals. Matthew, knowing that the Jews were eagerly looking forward to the coming of the Messiah promised in the Old Testament, presents Jesus as that Messiah. Luke, writing to a cultured people—the Greeks, whose ideal was the perfect Man, makes his Gospel center around Christ as the expression of that ideal. Mark writes to the Romans, a people whose ideal was power and service, so he pictures Christ to them as the Mighty Conqueror. John has in mind the needs of Christians of all nations, so he presents the deeper truths of the Gospel, among which we may mention the teachings concerning the deity of Christ and the Holy Spirit. The principle of adaptation referred to here was mentioned by Paul in 1 Cor. 9:19–21, and was illustrated in his ministry among Jew and Gentile. (Compare his message to the Jews in Acts 13:14–41, and that to the Greeks in

17:22–31.) This adaptation is a fine indication of a Divine design in the four Gospels.

In this connection we must remember that since humanity is just the same in one age as in another the message of the Gospels is addressed to mankind in general.

The foregoing facts reveal another reason for the writing of four Gospels; namely, that one gospel would not have been sufficient to present the many-sidedness of Christ's person. Each of the evangelists views Him from a different aspect. Matthew presents Him as King, Mark as Conqueror (and Servant), Luke as Son of Man, and John as Son of God. This viewing of Christ is like the viewing of a huge building—only one side can be taken in at one time.

The fact that the evangelists wrote their records from different viewpoints will explain the differences between them, their omissions and additions, the occasional seeming contradiction, and their lack of chronological order. The writers did not attempt to produce a **complete** biography of Christ, but taking into consideration the needs and character of the people to whom they were writing, they selected just those incidents and discourses which would emphasize their particular message. For example, Matthew, writing for the Jew, makes everything in his Gospel—the selection of discourses and incidents, the omissions and additions, the grouping of events—serve to stress the fact of Jesus' messiahship.

As an illustration of the way each evangelist emphasizes some particular aspect of Christ's person, let us take the following: Four authors undertake to write a biography of a person who has acquired fame as a statesman, soldier and author. One might wish to emphasize his political career, so he would gather together records of his campaigns and speeches to incorporate in the biography. Another would lay stress on his literary successes, and would describe his different writings. The third, with the thought in view of emphasizing his prowess in the military world, would describe his promotions, his decorations, and the battles in which he distinguished himself. The fourth might wish to enhance his virtues as manifested in home-life, so he would relate those incidents that would tend to set him forth as the ideal parent, husband, or friend.

The first three Gospels are called synoptical, because they give us a synopsis (common view) of the same events and have a common plan. The Gospel of John is written on an entirely different plan from the other three.

The following are the points of difference between the Synoptics and the Gospel of John:

1. The Synoptics contain an evangelistic message for unspiritual men; John contains a spiritual message for Christians.

2. In the three, we are taken over the ground of His Galilean ministry; but in the fourth, over the ground of His Judean ministry mainly.

3. In the three, His more public life is displayed; but in the fourth, we are shown His private life.

4. In the three, we are impressed with His real and perfect humanity; in the fourth, with His true and awful deity.

MATTHEW

Theme. The central theme of this Gospel is, Jesus the Messiah-King. Matthew, writing to the Jews, and knowing their great hopes, sets forth Jesus as the One fulfilling the Old Testament Scriptures relative to the Messiah. By the use of numerous Old Testament quotations, he shows what the Messiah ought to be; by a record of the words and deeds of Jesus, he proves that He was that Messiah. The frequent recurrence of the words "kingdom" and "kingdom of heaven" reveals another important theme of Matthew's Gospel. He sets forth the kingdom of heaven as promised in the Old Testament (Matt. 11:13), as proclaimed by John the Baptist and Jesus (3:2; 4:17), represented now by the Church (16:18, 19), and as triumphant at Jesus' second coming (25:31, 34).

Author. Reliable tradition credits Matthew with the writing of this book. Very little is said concerning him in the New Testament. We learn that he was a tax-gatherer under the Roman government but was called by the Lord to be a disciple and apostle.

To Whom Written. To all mankind in general, but to the Jews in particular. That it was intended primarily for the Jew may be seen by the following facts:

1. The great number of Old Testament quotations—there are about 60. One preaching to the Jews would have to prove his doctrine from the ancient Scriptures. Matthew makes these quotations the very basis of his Gospel.

2. The first words of the book "The book of the generations of Jesus Christ the son of David, the son of Abraham," would suggest immediately to the Jew, those two covenants that contained promises of the Messiah—the Davidic and the Abrahamic. 2 Sam. 7:8–16; Gen. 12:1–3.

3. There is a complete absence of explanations of Jewish customs showing that he was writing to a people acquainted with them.

CONTENTS

I.   The Advent of the Messiah. Chaps. 1:1 to 4:11.

1. Genealogy (1:1–17)
2. Birth (1:18–25)
3. The Wise Men (2:1–12)
4. Flight to Egypt and Return (2:13–23)
5. Baptism of Jesus (Chap. 3)
6. Temptation of Jesus (4:1–11)

The Jews paid great attention to genealogies. Before a person could be ordained to the priesthood, he was required to prove his descent from Aaron. In the time of Ezra some were rejected because of their failure to prove their right to the priesthood. Matthew, setting forth Jesus as Messiah, is obliged to prove from the Old Testament that He is Son of David—the One having a right to be king of Israel. Ps. 132:11. This he does in the genealogy found in Chap. 1:1–17, which is that of Joseph.

The Old Testament teaches that Messiah is to be born of a virgin, and that He must be, not only the Son of David, but the Son of God. Isa. 9:6. Matthew then records the virgin birth of Christ to show how these scriptures were fulfilled in Him.

The Wise Men are believed to have been a priestly tribe of Medes, whose chief functions were the study of astrology and the interpretation of dreams. They are representative of that class of Gentiles who worship the true God according to all the light they have. They may have been led to look for Messiah's coming by the testimony of the Jews living in their country.

Herod, though an able king, was a monster of cruelty. Knowing his own unpopularity and constantly fearing the loss of his throne, he ruthlessly destroyed any whom he suspected in the least of aspiring to rulership. This will explain his perturbation at the news of the birth of a king of the Jews, and his act of slaying the children of

Bethlehem. His murderous plan to kill the infant Christ was thwarted by a Divine warning.

Chapter 3 records the ministry of John the Baptist. His ministry was to prepare the nation for the coming of the Messiah, by the rite of baptism, which rite was symbolical of the cleansing from sin to be effected by the death of Messiah. The question arises here, Why was Jesus baptized, since He did not require repentance? Verse 15 will give us one answer: "For thus it becometh us to fulfill all righteousness." This signifies that Jesus wished to identify himself with the Jewish nation and take upon himself the obligation of keeping the whole law. See Gal. 4:4. From the Gospel of John we learn that another reason for Jesus' baptism was that John the Baptist might have a revelation of His deity. John 1:31, 33.

Since Christ came as a representative of humanity and since His mission was to destroy the works of the devil, it was fitting that He should begin His ministry by a victory over the great adversary of the race. Chapter 4 records His great triumph. One writer has remarked that Satan did not corner Christ, but Christ cornered Satan.

CHAPTER II

MATTHEW (CONTINUED)

II. The Ministry of the Messiah Chaps. 4:12–16:12.

1. Starting point of ministry; first disciples; first works (4:12–25)
2. The laws of Messiah's Kingdom—the Sermon on the Mount (Chap. 5 to 7)
3. Messiah's power manifested over disease, nature, demons, and death (Chap. 8 to 9:35)
4. The sending out of the twelve apostles (9:36 to 11:1)
5. John the Baptist's question (11:2–30)
6. Opposition of Pharisees (12:1–45)
7. Teaching in parables (Chap. 13)
8. Herod's opposition; feeding of 5,000 Chap. 14
9. Opposition from leaders in Judea and Galilee (15:1 to 16:12)

Matthew shows Galilee to be the starting point of Jesus' ministry in fulfillment of prophecy. Notice how often the expression "that it might be fulfilled" occurs in this Gospel. Jesus takes up John the Baptist's message; namely, the coming of the kingdom of heaven. By the expression "Kingdom of Heaven" we mean God's rule in and through Christ. This was promised in the Old Testament, is represented now by the church, and will be triumphant at Christ's second coming.

Having proclaimed the nearness of His kingdom, Jesus explains its laws in that discourse known as the Sermon on the Mount. There we learn about the character of the members of that kingdom (5:1–16), the principles governing it (5:17 to 7:6), and requirements for entering it (7:7–29).

Matthew now shows Jesus presenting His credentials to the nation; i.e., manifesting His power as a proof of His messiahship. But though the miracles were signs of His deity and proofs of His mission, they were never performed for mere display or to satisfy curiosity, but for the relief of suffering humanity. We may regard His miracles as symbols of His saving power.

1. His power over disease symbolized His power over sin.
2. His power over demons was typical of the complete overthrow of Satan's kingdom.
3. His power over death reveals Him as the One who will quicken all the dead.
4. His power over nature shows Him as the One who shall deliver the whole earth from the curse.

Jesus has already chosen some disciples. 4:18–22. No doubt many more have gathered about Him. Out of these He chooses twelve to help Him in preaching the Gospel, and to train them for their future work as leaders of the church. For the purpose of confirming their message, He imparts the power to work miracles. Since the time of Gentile evangelization has not yet come, He limits their ministry to Israel. 10:6.

The Jews' conception of the Messiah was that of a mighty prince who would set up a great temporal kingdom. Jesus did not measure up to their ideals for He proclaimed the coming of a spiritual kingdom. Though John the Baptist's conception of the Messiah was a spiritual one, it is possible that he expected Messiah's kingdom to be set up immediately with power. Feeling disappointed in his expectations, and seeing no signs of the Messiah's delivering him from prison, he yields to doubt and despondency. But fortunately he takes his doubts to Jesus, who quickly confirms his faith.

Chapter twelve records the Pharisees' opposition to Jesus. Their reasons for opposing Him were as follows: His lowly origin; His consorting with sinners; and His opposing their traditions. Chapter 12 describes opposition for the last-named reason. The Pharisees, though accepting the whole of the Old Testament, accepted as authoritative a mass of tradition which obscured the true meaning of the Scriptures. In verses 1–13 the Sabbath question is dealt with. By their traditional interpretation, the Jewish teachers had made this day of rest a burden to man, whereas God had intended it to be a blessing. Because His disciples plucked kernels of wheat on the Sabbath, and because He himself healed a man on that day, He was accused of breaking the law. In His answer our Lord taught that the Sabbath gives way before human necessity (vv. 3, 4, 12); that God desires practical goodness rather than outward observances (v. 7); and that He, as Lord of the Sabbath, had the right to decide how it should be kept (v. 8). In their bitterness to Jesus the Pharisees went the length of accusing Him of performing His works by the power of Satan, whereupon the Lord uttered a warning against blaspheming the Spirit.

Up to this point our Lord had been teaching in plain language, but on seeing the opposition to His message, He began teaching in parables when speaking of His Kingdom. He did this to prevent their distorting His words and using them against Him. See Luke 23:2. (A parable is a story which teaches a heavenly truth by using an earthly illustration.) His object in thus doing was to conceal the truth from the mocker and the opposer (13:13–15), and to reveal it to the earnest seeker (vv. 11, 16). The general truths taught in the parables are that during the absence of Christ, the whole world will not be converted, that not all the Gospel seed sown will bear fruit; that good and evil will continue side by side until the second coming of Christ. The parables are intended to show the growth and development of the Church during this dispensation and its relation to sinners, professors, and the world in general.

Chapter 15:1–20 records further opposition of the leaders toward Jesus. They accuse Him of transgressing their traditions, whereupon in stern language He rebukes them for burying the true interpretation of Scripture beneath man-made traditions. In response to their request for a sign (16:1), He points them to signs of the times; i.e., the ripeness of the nation for judgment, the presence in their midst of preachers proclaiming the kingdom of God, and the working of the supernatural. Jesus had already given them signs (Matt. 11:5), but they want something spectacular. Since Christ always performed His miracles for the relief of suffering humanity, He refuses their request.

III. The Claim of the Messiah. Chaps. 16:13 to 23:39.

1. His claim before the disciples (16:13 to 20:28)
2. His claim before the nation (20:29 to 23:39)

Thus far Jesus has not measured up to the people's ideal of the Messiah, for instead of proclaiming a temporal kingdom, He has been proclaiming a spiritual one. But though the people do not accept Him as Messiah, they consider Him a great prophet (16:13). Because of the people's attitude, Jesus does not make a public proclamation of His Messiahship, for to do so would lead the Jews to look for the setting up of an earthly kingdom and their deliverance from the Romans. Because of this He makes His claim in private to His disciples (16:15–19) and forbids them to tell anyone that He is the Messiah (v. 20). Following He makes known the means by which His kingdom is to be ushered in; namely, through His death and resurrection (16:21). Peter, sharing the common views of the people cannot conceive of a suffering and dying Messiah and tries to dissuade Jesus from submitting to death. Jesus rebukes him, and teaches the disciples that before the crown comes the cross (16:24–27). Verse 28 of the same chapter refers to the transfiguration, which was a fore-gleaming of Christ's entering into His glory.

The news of His coming humiliation and death has so disheartened the disciples that, in order to encourage them, He allows them to see Him for a short time in His glorified state, and to hear the voice of the Father approving His purpose. This takes place at the transfiguration (Chap. 17). Notice that He charges His disciples to maintain silence concerning this event in order not to raise false hopes among the people (v. 9). He later repeats the prophecy of His coming death (17:23) in order to impress that fact on the minds of His disciples.

Though Jesus has not made public proclamation of His messiahship, it is necessary, in order that the Scriptures be fulfilled, and that the nation have an opportunity of accepting or rejecting Him, that He make some kind of public claim. This took place at the triumphal entry in Jerusalem (21:1–16). But notice that this was not a warlike demonstration, but the peaceful entry of a King, "**meek** and sitting upon an ass, and a colt the foal of an ass" (21:5). As such it was not calculated to alarm the Romans who were always fearing an uprising, neither did it cause the nation at large to believe that Jesus was the great conquering Messiah they were expecting. Those who acclaimed Jesus at this time were mostly His disciples and those who had benefited by His ministry.

Jesus' claims are rejected by the nation as represented by the leaders (21:15, 23, 32, 45, 46; 22:15–40). Following this He foretells, in parables, the rejection of the Jewish nation by God and His turning to the Gentiles (the Parables of the Wicked Husbandman and the Marriage Supper). Chapter 23 marks Jesus' final break with the religious leaders, and His weeping over Jerusalem.

IV. The Sacrifice of the Messiah. Chaps. 24 to 27.

1. Discourse Concerning Christ's Second Coming (24:1–41)
2. Judgments to Take Place at the Second Coming (21:42 To 25–46)
3. Betrayal, Arrest, and Trial of Jesus (Chap. 26)
4. The Crucifixion (Chap. 27)

Concerning Christ's discourse in 24:1–41, we quote from Professor Moorehead:

Two supreme objects occupy the field of this marvelous prophecy, one of which lies near to the Divine speaker, and the other remote from Him in point of view. But both are perfectly clear to His omniscient vision. The near is the fall of Jerusalem, the remote is His second advent. The first took place within forty years after the prediction—viz., 70 AD; the second is still future. The one was restricted to a very limited area, though it affected the whole world in its issues; the other embraces the planet.

Some of the predictions apply to both these events but in different degrees. The fall of Jerusalem is insignificant in comparison with the coming of the Lord Jesus Christ. Yet there is a striking resemblance between these two events; the destruction of the Holy City prefigures the more tremendous scenes which are to accompany the advent of the Lord. The one answers to the other as type to antitype.

To illustrate: In chapter 24:14, our Lord says, "And this gospel of the kingdom shall be preached in all the world for a witness unto all nations; and then shall the end come." That this prediction was fulfilled before Jerusalem's destruction Paul attests. Col. 1:6, 23. The like world-wide proclamation is immediately to precede the final. Rev. 14:6, 7. So likewise the unequaled tribulation spoken of in 24:21 appears to belong to both the events referred to. That scenes of suffering, horror and crime almost indescribable took place at the siege and capture of Jerusalem by the Roman army is well known. But that another "time of trouble," an unparalleled tribulation immediately precedes the advent is certain. (Compare Matt. 24:21, 29; Dan. 12:1, 2; Jer. 30:7.) Israel and the Gentiles alike will be in the tribulation.

Notice the Judgments mentioned in 24:42 to 25:46. Judgment on unwatchful servants (24:42–51); judgment on unprepared servants (25:1–13); judgment on unprofitable servants (25:14–30); judgment on the nations (25:14–46).

Isaiah's prophecy of the suffering Messiah (Isa. 53), finds its fulfillment in Chaps. 26, 27.

V. The Triumph of the Messiah. Chap. 28.

The Gospel of Matthew reaches a happy consummation in the resurrection of the Messiah from the dead. All power is given to Him in heaven and in earth, for this reason He is able to send His followers into all the world with the message of salvation. Thus are fulfilled the words of Isaiah, "Behold my servant whom I uphold; mine elect in whom my soul delighteth; I have put my Spirit upon him; **he shall bring forth judgment to the Gentiles** . . . he shall not fail nor be discouraged till he have set judgment in the earth: and **the isles shall wait for his law.**" Isa. 42:1, 4. "It is a light thing that thou shouldest be my servant to raise up the tribes of Jacob, and to restore the preserved of Israel; I will also give thee for a light to the Gentiles, **that thou mayest be my salvation to the ends of the earth.**" Isa. 49:6.

For the purpose of fixing the contents of Matthew in his mind, let the student learn the following chapter and word outline:

1. Genealogy and birth.
2. Flight.
3. Baptism.
4. Temptation.
5–7. Sermon on the Mount.
8–9. Miracles.
10. The Twelve Sent Forth.
11–12. Discourses.
13. Parables.
14–15. Feeding the multitude.
16. Peter's Confession.
17. Transfiguration.
18–20. Discourses.
21. Triumphal Entry.
22. Plots of Enemy.
23. Woes.
24–25. Second Coming.
26. Betrayal.
27. Crucifixion.
28. Resurrection.

CHAPTER III

MARK

Theme. Written for a military people (the Romans), the Gospel of Mark gives a brief narrative of that three years' campaign of the Captain of our salvation, carried on and completed for the deliverance of our souls and the defeat of Satan, by His (Christ's) labors, sufferings, death, resurrection and final triumph. In this narrative, Jesus is set forth as the mighty Conqueror.

Author. Mark was the son of Mary, a woman of Jerusalem, whose house was open to the early Christians. Acts 12:12. He accompanied Paul and Barnabas on their first missionary tour. The contemplation of the dangers facing the party as they journeyed to unknown regions, seems to have unnerved him so that he returned to Jerusalem. Acts 13:13. Later, Barnabas' proposal to take Mark with him on their second tour brought about a sharp contention between him and Paul. The apostle, viewing the matter from the standpoint of good judgment, thought it best not to take with them one who had proved himself to be a "slacker." The sympathetic Barnabas thought that Mark should have an opportunity to redeem himself, so separating himself from Paul he took him with him to Cyprus (Acts 15:36–41). John Mark justified the confidence of Barnabas in him, for later records show that he made a success in the ministry. Peter makes favorable mention of him (1 Pet. 5:13) and Paul changed his opinion concerning him to the extent of writing: "Take Mark and bring him with thee; for he is profitable to me for the ministry" (2 Tim. 4:11).

The abundant testimony of the Church Fathers makes it fairly certain that Mark accompanied Peter to Rome as his interpreter, and that he compiled this gospel from Peter's preaching. His Roman name—Mark—seems to point to the fact that he was brought up in Roman circles. These facts would make him peculiarly fitted to write a gospel for the Romans.

To Whom Written. The following facts will indicate how the gospel is adapted to the Romans in particular:

1. The briefness of the gospel, its vivid depicting of scenes marked by energy and movement reveal it as peculiarly adapted to such an active, energetic people as the Romans. The main characteristic of this book is the constant recurrence of the words "straightway," and "forthwith," conveying the idea of military activity and promptness. One writer has remarked that the style of Mark resembles that used by Julius Caesar in his history of some of his campaigns.

2. Money is reduced to Roman currency.

3. Roman division of time is used.

4. Explanation of Hebrew customs are given (7:3, 4). This shows, at least, that the book was written to Gentiles.

5. There are practically no references to O. T. prophecies after Chapter 1. The Romans, who were unacquainted with those Scriptures would not be likely to understand them.

CONTENTS

Since Mark contains the same matter as Matthew (though in different arrangement), we will not give an extended outline. We suggest that the student read the entire book and then learn the following analysis.

Keeping in mind that Mark is portraying Christ as the mighty Conqueror, let us go through the gospel and see how this thought is carried out.

First of all, Mark describes the coming of the great Conqueror by recording—

1. His name and heralding (1:1–8)
2. His initial victory over Satan (1:9–13)
3. The first proclamation of His kingdom (1:14–20
4. His first works of power (1:21 to 2:12)

He describes the conflict of the mighty King by exhibiting Him as—

1. Enlisting subjects for His kingdom—apostles, publicans and sinners, the sick and needy. 2:13 to 3:35.
2. Explaining the growth of His kingdom. 4:1–34.
3. Conquering nature, demons, disease and death. 4:35 to 5:43.
4. Opposed by the people (6:1–6), Herod (6:14:29), and by the scribes and Pharisees (7:1–23; 8:10–21).

He exhibits the Conqueror claiming His right to the kingdom of power and presents Him—

1. Teaching His followers how victory was to be won in His kingdom—by suffering and death. 8:31–38; 10:28–45.
2. Claiming His right to the kingdom, in Jerusalem, by His triumphal entry (11:1–11), by His cleansing of the temple (11:15–19), by His defeat of those leaders who questioned His authority (11: 27 to 12:44), and by the prophecy of His coming again in glory (13:1–37).

Mark shows how Christ prepares for the setting up of His kingdom by His

1. Preparing for death (14:1–72)
2. Yielding to death (15:1–47)

Finally he shows Jesus taking the kingdom (spiritual) by His—

1. Conquering death (16:1–14)
2. Sending His followers to proclaim His triumph (16:15–20)

LUKE

Theme. Luke's Gospel gives us a historical narrative setting forth Jesus Christ as the perfect Divine Man. Luke wrote especially for the Greek people whose mission was to improve man morally, intellectually, and physically, and whose ideal was the perfect man. Just as the Jews failed to attain to salvation through the law and its ceremonies, so the Greeks failed to do so through their culture and philosophy. Education was for the Greeks what the law was for the Jews—it was their schoolmaster to bring them to Christ. Seeing their inability to save humanity by their learning, many philosophers among the Greeks saw that their only hope of salvation was the coming of a divine man. Luke, to meet the need of the Greek, sets forth Jesus as the perfect Divine Man, the representative and Saviour of humanity.

Author. Luke, a companion of Paul the apostle. Col. 4:14; Philemon 24; 2 Tim. 4:11. Christian writers of the early centuries tell us that Luke wrote the Gospel that bears his name; that it was substantially the same which he and Paul had preached among the Greeks; and that it was produced and published among the Greek people.

To Whom Written. The Gospel of Luke is addressed to the Greeks in particular. Dr. Gregory tells us that it is suited to the Greeks in various ways:

1. In authorship. It is thought that Luke was a Greek. He was a highly educated man, indicated by the fact that he was a physician and by the style of his writing.

2. In plan. It is considered the most orderly history of the sayings and doings of Jesus. By careful reading we find passages that are written by a thoughtful man to a meditative and philosophic people.

3. In style. Luke's gospel is peculiarly attractive because of its poetic eloquence. Note the songs given in the first chapter. Throughout the gospel we find the **discourses** of Jesus recorded in direct contrast to Mark's Gospel which laid emphasis on the **deeds** of Jesus rather than His teachings.

4. Its omissions. Portions that are distinctly Jewish are omitted. Little or nothing is said about Old Testament prophecy.

CONTENTS

Luke contains many incidents and discourses found in Matthew and Mark. We shall deal, therefore with only those details that are not found in the other Gospels.

I. The Introduction. Chaps. 1:1–4.

As was common with Greek historians, Luke begins His Gospel, with a preface. He tells us that many in his time had undertaken to write an account of Christ's ministry (v. 1). Dissatisfied evidently with these attempts, he undertakes to write an account of the Lord's life "in order." He states his qualifications for undertaking such a work; namely, the fact of his having received his information from eyewitnesses (v. 2), and his having a perfect knowledge of all the facts of the Lord's life and ministry from the very beginning (v. 3). He then dedicates his Gospel to one Theophilus for the purpose of confirming his faith (v. 4).

II. The Advent of the Divine Man. Chaps. 1:5 to 4:13

Under this heading we shall study the following details that are not found in the other Gospels:

1. The annunciation of John the Baptist's birth (1:5–25)
2. The annunciation of Jesus' birth to Mary (26–38)
3. Mary's visit to Elisabeth (1:39–55)
4. The birth and childhood of John the Baptist (1:56–80)
5. The journey to Bethlehem (2:1–7)
6. The message of the angels (2:8–20)
7. The circumcision of Jesus and His presentation in the temple (2:21–39)
8. Jesus' childhood (2:40–52)
9. The genealogy of Jesus (3:23–38)

Luke opens his narrative with an event not found in other Gospels—the annunciation of the birth of John the Baptist. His father, who was a priest, was performing his ministry in the temple, which at that particular time was the offering up of incense. The office of incensing was held so honorable that no one was allowed to perform it twice, since it brought the officiating priest nearer the Divine presence in the Holy of Holies than any other priestly act. The rising cloud of incense was a symbol of Israel's prayers arising to God. While engaged in this ministry an angel appeared and announced the coming birth of a son. It should be noted that this annunciation was the first recorded Divine message since the time of the prophet Malachi (about 400 BC). Whom did Malachi's last message mention? Mal. 4:5. Whom did the angel mention in his message? Luke 1:17.

Then follows the annunciation to Mary. Note that Matthew records the annunciation to Joseph. Matthew gives the story from Joseph's viewpoint; Luke, from Mary's. The fact that Luke is telling the story from Mary's viewpoint, furnishes us with a good reason for believing that the genealogy given by Luke is that of Mary.

Mary, probably at the suggestion of the angel (1:36) visits her cousin Elisabeth. In response to her salutation, she gives utterance to that beautiful song commonly known as the "Magnificat" (1:46–55). This song is based on Old Testament Scriptures. (See Gen. 30:13 and 1 Sam. 2:1–10.)

John the Baptist is born. Contrary to the usual custom among the Jews, he is not named after a dead relative. His name means "The Lord is gracious"—an appropriate name for the forerunner of the Lord of grace. Zacharias' tongue is loosened, and, filled with the Spirit of God, he praises God in that song commonly known as the "Benedictus" (1:68–79).

Matthew records the simple fact that Christ was born at Bethlehem. Luke goes into details, and records the circumstances that led to Joseph and Mary's taking the journey to that town; namely, a Roman registration for taxing, which required the presence of each person in his native town. Who preached the first Gospel message (2:10–12)? Who were the first evangelists (2:15–17)?

Paul tells us in Galatians 4:4 that God's Son was made "under the law;" i.e., He fulfilled its requirements. So we see His parents in Luke 2:21–24 fulfilling the law in regard to Him in the performance of two ceremonies—that of circumcision and presentation to the Lord. By the former, He became a member of the Jewish nation, and by the latter

Jehovah's claim upon Him as the first-born of the family was recognized. (See Ex. 13:2–15; 34:19.)

Luke is the only Evangelist who records any incident of Jesus' childhood. He does so in order to emphasize His humanity—to set Him forth as the "Seed of the woman." Gen. 3:15. He wishes to show that though Jesus was the Son of God, He grew in a natural way (2:40, 52). He records Jesus' visit to Jerusalem in order to show that Jesus, from childhood, had a consciousness of His Divine mission (2:49).

Luke, like Matthew, records a genealogy of Jesus. But on examination it will be seen that they differ. Matthew traces Jesus' descent through David's son **Solomon** (Matt. 1:6); Luke, through David's son Nathan (Luke 3:31). The simple explanation is that the one in Matthew is that of Joseph; that in Luke, of Mary. Matthew shows that Jesus had the **legal right** to the throne of David; this makes Him David's heir. But since the Messiah must be the seed of David **according to the flesh**, and since Jesus' was not Joseph's real son it follows that His **natural** right to the throne must be proved. Since it is Luke's purpose to emphasize the humanity of Christ—to set Him forth as the Seed of woman, and since He describes the birth of Christ from Mary's viewpoint, we conclude that the genealogy given in Luke is that of Mary, given to prove that Jesus had the **natural right** to David's throne by being born of a virgin of the house of David. It may be objected that Luke 3:23 shows Joseph to be the son of Heli and that Mary is not mentioned. This may be explained by the fact that among the Jews the descent was not reckoned through the wife, so that Joseph, though really the son-in-law of Heli, is reckoned as his son.

CHAPTER IV

LUKE (CONTINUED)

III. His Ministry in Galilee. Chaps. 4:14 to 9:50

This section contains the following details peculiar to Luke:

1. The first rejection at Nazareth (4:14–30)
2. The miraculous draught of fishes (5:1–11)
3. The raising of the widow's son (7:11–18)
4. The anointing of Jesus by a sinful woman (7:36–50)
5. The women who ministered to the Lord (8:1–3)
6. Zeal without knowledge rebuked (9:49, 50)

Chapter 4:14–32 records Jesus' first rejection at Nazareth. After the successful beginning of His ministry (Matt. 4:23–25), He returns to His native town. Sabbath finds Him attending the synagogue. After the reading of the Scriptures it was the custom to call upon some teacher or preacher, if one were present, to deliver a message. (Compare Acts 13:15.) The leader, having heard of Jesus' ministry, calls Him to the pulpit. Taking as His text Isaiah 61:1, our Lord sits down (after the manner of oriental teachers) and preaches that text as being fulfilled in Him. The people at first are moved by His gracious words, but later stumbled over the fact that He was only the Son of Joseph. How could He, the son of a carpenter, be the fulfillment of the Scriptures? Jesus reminds them that a prophet is usually not accepted in his own country and illustrates this by citing two Old Testament incidents where, God's prophets, unappreciated in general by Israel, were received by the Gentiles. The action of the people shows that they understood this as an implied reference to their rejection and the Gentiles' reception.

Luke supplements Matthew's account of the calling of the first disciples (Matt. 4:17–22) by recording a miracle in that connection—namely the miraculous draught of fishes. Such a revelation of Christ's power brings Peter to his knees in deep conviction of his own sinfulness. This miracle may be considered as typical of Peter's great draught on the day of Pentecost. (Compare Luke 5:10; Acts 2:41.)

A funeral at Nain gives the Lord an opportunity to reveal himself as the One who "shall wipe away all tears" (Rev. 21:4).

While Jesus was seated in the house of a Pharisee, a woman who had been a great sinner, comes and anoints Him. The Pharisee, who considered the touch of such a woman defiling, is surprised. Jesus, in the parable of the Two Debtors, teaches Simon that the attentions of this woman were bestowed upon Him in gratitude for sins forgiven. Simon, He said, had not given Him these attentions. This statement is a thrust at the self-righteous Pharisee for it implies that he had not felt the burden of sin as the woman had, and therefore felt no gratitude.

In chapter 8:1–3, Luke gives us an insight into the ministry of women in relation to the Lord. He mentions some who helped to support Him.

Our Lord teaches His disciples a lesson in tolerance (9:49, 50). We here see the other side of the "beloved disciple's" character. Though loving and gentle, he was at the same time zealous, and had a hatred for anything he believed to be wrong.

IV. His Ministry in Perea. Chaps. 9:51 to 19:28

In this section we notice the following details peculiar to Luke:

1. Jesus' rejection by the Samaritans (9:51–56)
2. The sending forth of the Seventy (10:1–12, 17–20)
3. The Good Samaritan (10:25–37)
4. Martha and Mary (10:38–42)
5. The Parable of the Rich Fool (12:13–21)
6. A lesson on repentance (13:1–9)
7. The healing of the woman with an infirmity (13:10–17)
8. Herod's warning (13:31–33)
9. Healing of the man with dropsy (14:1–6)
10. True hospitality, and the parable of the Great Supper (14:7–24)
11. Discourse on counting the cost (14:25–33)
12. Parables of grace and warning (15:8 to 16:15)
13. The Rich Man and Lazarus (16:19–31)
14. A lesson on faith (17:5–10)
15. The ten lepers (17:11–19)
16. Parables of the Unjust Judge and of the Pharisee and the Publican (18:1–14)
17. The conversion of Zaccheus (19:1–10)
18. Parable of the Pounds (19:11–27)

The prejudice of the Samaritans toward the Jews is seen in their refusal to receive Jesus because His face was set towards Jerusalem. John and James, the "Sons of Thunder" (Mark 3:17), in an overzealous spirit, wish to emulate Elijah's example in calling down fire from heaven. This zeal without knowledge receives a severe rebuke from the **Master**.

Besides sending forth twelve apostles, Jesus sent forth a large party of seventy disciples. Such a large number was necessary because the time for the Lord's departure was at hand, and the large territory of Perea was yet unevangelized. Their instructions are similar to those of the Twelve.

Jesus takes advantage of a question put to Him by a Jewish lawyer to strike a blow at Jewish prejudice. In answer to the man's question, Who is my neighbor? Jesus utters the parable of the Good Samaritan, choosing as an example of the perfect neighbor, one of a race hated by the Jews. The lesson contained in the parable is that anybody in need, be he Jew or Gentile, is our neighbor.

Chapter 10:38–42 gives a little insight into the social life of Jesus, describing two intimate friends of His—Martha and Mary. It is interesting to note here how much Luke emphasizes the ministry of women in his gospel. (See also Luke 1:26–55; 2:36; 8:1–3.)

In the parable of the Rich Fool the Lord sounds out a warning against covetousness.

Jesus is referred to certain calamities which had befallen the Galileans, the inference drawn from these calamities being that they were the result of sin on the part of the people (13:1–10). Our Lord taught His informants that exceptional suffering was not necessarily the result of exceptional sin, and that they, if they did not repent, would perish. To show the longsuffering of God toward Israel and toward sinners in general, He utters the parable of the Barren Fig Tree.

Jesus' method of dealing with merely speculative questions is seen in 13:23–30. The disciples raise the question as to the number of those who will be saved. Instead of giving a direct answer Jesus warns them to see to it that they themselves were found in the narrow way that leads to life everlasting.

Herod, ruler of Galilee and Perea, fearing that the immense crowds that Jesus was drawing might cause a disturbance in his territory, employs some Pharisees to warn Jesus to leave his dominions. Seeing through the scheme of the "Fox," Jesus assures him that he has nothing to fear from Him since He is working for the relief of humanity. Herod need not seek to kill Him; Jerusalem, "the prophet's slaughter-house" will do that. At the remembrance of Jerusalem, Christ breaks forth into tears, and prophesies its destruction (13:31–35).

Our Lord, teaching a lesson on true hospitality, counsels His hearers to invite to their feast the poor and needy, for which acts of charity, they would be rewarded at the resurrection of the just (14:12–14). On hearing of that resurrection, one of the company breaks forth into an exclamation of joy at the happy prospect of the coming of God's kingdom (v. 15). Jesus takes advantage of this utterance to teach, that blessed as that event will be, many will refuse the invitation to the Great Supper (vv. 16–24).

Verses 25–35 of chapter 14 show how Jesus treated prospective disciples. He did not promise them a life of ease, but required the most severe self-denial. His measure of a disciple was the cross.

In answer to the taunt of the Pharisees charging Him with consorting with sinners, Jesus utters the parables of the Lost Sheep, the Lost Coin, and the Prodigal Son, to teach the love of God toward sinners (Chap. 15). Notice that all these parables contain the same line of thought; namely, loss, restoration, and joy. Chapter 16 contains the parables of the Unjust Steward, and the incident of the Rich Man and Lazarus. The former is intended to teach Christians foresight in relation to money matters. A dishonest steward is about to be dismissed from his position. Unwilling to work and ashamed to beg, he resolves to use his master's money in such a way that it will ensure him a happy future. The application is as follows: Christians are stewards; i.e., they are entrusted with their Master's property. The time is coming when their stewardship will cease (through death). Because of this, they should so use their money on earth (by supporting missions, etc.), that when they reach heaven, they may enjoy an eternal interest on their investments. (Compare Luke 16:9 and 1 Tim. 6:17, 18.) The incident of the Rich Man and Lazarus shows the fate of those who, unmindful of the **sufferings** of their neighbor, live entirely for self.

An injunction to forgiveness on the part of Christ (17:1–4) leads the disciples to desire a deeper spiritual experience—namely, an increase of faith (v. 5). They have in mind the **quantity** of faith; Jesus emphasizes its **quality**, showing the efficacy of faith as small as a mustard seed. Then He proceeds to teach them that though they might have the faith that would pluck up sycamine trees, they were not to glory in it, but rather consider themselves unprofitable servants (v. 10); for to believe God is only their duty.

Luke's Gospel is the Gospel of humanity. He emphasizes in his choice of parables, God's love for all mankind. It is interesting to note how he stresses Jesus' love for the Samaritans—a people hated and despised by the Jews. (See 9:52–56; 10:25–37.) In the incident of the healing of the ten lepers (17:11–19), he uses the ingratitude of the Jewish lepers as a dark background for the faith and thankfulness of one Samaritan (vv. 17, 18).

To teach importunity in prayer, Jesus utters the parable of the Unjust Judge. The lesson is: If an **unjust** judge will be moved by the importunity of a woman in whom he feels no interest how much more will God, the **righteous** judge, respond to the prayers of those whom He loves. The parable of the Pharisee and the Publican is a fine illustration of Romans 3:19–21.

Chapter 19:1–10 records the conversion of a member of that despised class—the publicans. The publicans were Jewish tax-gatherers in the employ of the Roman government. Because of their serving the

Jews' oppressors, and the fact that they were usually dishonest, they were hated by the people. Zaccheus manifested the genuineness of his conversion by an offer of complete restitution of all he acquired dishonest means.

Is the parable of the Talents (19:11–28) the same as that parable found in Matthew 25:14–30? Compare them.

V. His Crucifixion and Resurrection.
Chaps. 19:29 to 24:53

We shall notice here the following details peculiar to Luke:
1. Christ's weeping over Jerusalem (19:41–44)
2. Strife among the disciples for chief positions (22:24–30)
3. Warning to Peter (22:31–34)
4. Instructions to disciples (22:35–38)
5. Jesus before Herod (23:8–12)
6. The lamentation of the women of Jerusalem (23:27–31)
7. The repentant thief (23:39–43)
8. The walk to Emmaus (24:13–35)
9. The command to tarry (24:49)

With what feelings does the Deity pronounce judgment? Our Lord's weeping over Jerusalem will answer the question. He prophesies its destruction by the Romans and attributes its coming calamities to spiritual ignorance—"Because thou knewest not the time of thy visitation."

In spite of their teaching by the Lord, the disciples were still dull of understanding. The fact of their striving among themselves for the greatest position in the kingdom shows that they had not clearly apprehended the true nature of that kingdom. The thought of a temporal kingdom still occupied their minds. Jesus takes advantage of this to bring home a lesson in humility.

Chapter 22:31, 32 gives us a glimpse behind the scenes and shows us the cause of Peter's great fall. His over-confidence had made it necessary for God to permit Satan to sift him. (Compare Satan's temptation of Job.) We also learn why Peter rose again after his fall—Christ prayed for him.

We offer a paraphrase of the words found in 22:35–38. Jesus as much as says to the disciples,

> When you went forth the first time, I was popular with the people, and consequently, you, My representatives lacked nothing. But conditions have changed. The nation is against Me; I am about to be crucified—to be 'reckoned among the transgressors.' Therefore you need not expect to be received kindly by the people. For this reason, provide yourselves with purse and scrip. As symbolical of the spiritual warfare you are about to be engaged in, provide yourselves with swords.

Pontius Pilate, having examined Jesus, and having learned that He is of Galilee, sends Him to Herod, the ruler of that province. Herod has heard of Jesus' miracles and is anxious to witness His power. He treats Him as He would treat a magician whose tricks he wished to witness. Jesus has nothing to say to this cruel ruler and maintains a dignified silence. Whereupon Herod and his soldiers mock and send Him back to Pilate.

On His way to the cross, Jesus is met by the women of Jerusalem who bewail Him. He tells them that He does not ask for their pity; rather, they are the ones to be pitied. For He asks them, if the innocent suffer, as He is about to, what will happen to the guilty (23:31)?

Matthew tells that both thieves, crucified with Christ, railed on Him. Luke adds one more detail and tells us that one of these repented. They offer a type of two classes of humanity in relation to Christ. Both were sinners, both condemned by the law, both paying the penalty of the law, and both were without hope, yet one is saved and the other lost. The destiny of these men was decided by their attitude to the innocent One hanging on the cross.

In chapter 24:13–35, we get an insight into the feelings of the disciples before the resurrection of Christ. The death of their Master had proved a great blow to them. Though He had prophesied His resurrection, they had not grasped fully the truth that the Messiah may first suffer and then rise again, so influenced were they by the Jewish idea that the coming of the Messiah could be nothing but a glorious one. In an exposition of the Old Testament that causes the hearts of the two disciples to burn, Jesus, who at first concealed His identity from them, showed them how it was necessary for the Messiah to suffer before entering into His glory.

Luke concludes his Gospel with the record of Jesus' command to the disciples to tarry, and His ascension. The record of events repeated in the first chapter of the book of Acts, is written by the same author.

CHAPTER V

JOHN 1 TO 6

Theme. The Gospel of John is an accumulation of testimony to prove that Jesus is the Christ, the Son of the living God. It was written by John in response to an appeal from the Church—already possessing the other gospels—for the deeper truths of the gospel, and written with a view to furthering the spiritual life of the Church. It contains the substance of John's preaching to the Church of those spiritual truths that he had received from the Lord. John's purpose in this gospel is to present Christ to all Christians as the incarnate Word of God.

Author. John the apostle. Reliable writers of the early centuries tell us that John wrote his Gospel at the end of the first century, and that it was substantially the embodiment of his preaching of the deeper truths that he had learned from intimate communion with Christ.

Of all the apostles, John enjoyed the closest intimacy with the Master. He belongs to the inner circle consisting of himself, Peter and James, the members of which alone Jesus permitted to be present during the great crises of His ministry—such as the transfiguration and the agony in Gethsemane. It was John who leaned upon his Master's breast during the Passover Supper; he it was, who, when the other disciples had fled, followed his Lord to the judgment (John 18:15); of all the apostles, he was the only one who stood by the cross to receive the Lord's dying message. John 19:25–27. This intimacy and communion with the Lord together with a half century of experience as a pastor and evangelist, well qualified him to write that Gospel which contains the most spiritual and sublime teachings concerning the person of Christ.

To Whom Written. To the Church in general. The Gospel of John was written many years later than the other Gospels. The latter, speaking generally, contained an evangelistic message for unspiritual men; they were missionary Gospels. After churches had been established by the labors of the apostles, there came a request from Christians everywhere for a statement of the deeper truths of the Gospel. To meet this demand, John wrote his Gospel.

That this Gospel was written primarily for Christians may be seen by the following facts:

1. The teaching it contains concerning some of the profoundest themes of the Gospel—the preexistence of Christ, His incarnation, His relation to the Father, the person and work of the Holy Spirit—indicate that it was written for spiritual people.

2. The writer takes for granted that those to whom he is writing are acquainted with the other three Gospels, for he omits most of the well-known incidents of the Lord's life, excepting, of course, those relating to the passion and resurrection, without which no gospel could be complete.

CONTENTS

   I. The Foreword. 1:1–18.
   II. Christ's Revelation to the World, by His Claims. 1:19 to 6:71.
   III. Rejection of Christ's Claims. 7:1 to 12:50.
   IV. Christ's Manifestation to His Disciples. Chaps. 13–17.
   V. Christ's Humiliation and Glorification. Chaps. 18–21.

I. The Foreword. Chap. 1:1–18.

   1. Christ's manifestation in eternity. 1:1–5.
   2. Christ's manifestation in time. 1:6–18.

The synoptics begin their history by recording the earthly origin of Christ. Matthew and Luke both record His virgin birth. John takes it for granted that Christians everywhere are acquainted with these facts, and omitting the record of His earthly origin, describes His heavenly origin. Although John does not give a direct account of the virgin birth of Christ, he refers indirectly to it in verse 14.

Notice the name by which John refers to Christ—the Word. Christ is called the Word, because, as our words are the expression of our thoughts and character, so Christ was the expression of God's thought for us and of His character, yea, of His very essence.

How did the world receive its Creator (v. 10)? Which may be called the saddest verse in the Bible (v. 11)? What was given to those who did receive Him? To what event does verse 14 refer (Compare Phil. 2:6–8)? What did John say the disciples received (v. 16; Compare Col. 1:19; 2:9)? What contrast is brought out in verse 17?

II. Christ's Manifestation to the World.
Chaps. 1:19 to 6:71.

1. John the Baptist's testimony. 1:19–34.
2. Testimony of the first disciples. 1:35–51.
3. The first miracle and first cleansing of the temple. Chap. 2.
4. Interview with Nicodemus. 3:1–21.
5. John's testimony to his disciples. 3:22–36.
6. Jesus' ministry in Samaria. 4:1–43.
7. The healing of the nobleman's son. 4:43–54.
8. The healing of the impotent man, followed by discourse. Chap. 5.
9. Feeding of the multitude; discourse on the Bread of Life. Chap. 6.

John, like the other evangelists, mentions the ministry of John the Baptist. Since the Baptist was attracting large crowds by his ministry and was ministering a rite which was new to the Jewish religion;—namely, baptism,—the Jewish authorities felt it their duty to investigate the claims of this new preacher. They sent a delegation to question him as to his identity and authority. He humbly confesses that he is nothing but a voice crying in the wilderness (1:23); that his mission is that of the engineers of that day before the coming of an Eastern king; namely, the preparing of the roads before him (1:23); that his baptism was only symbolical and typical of the baptism to be administered by the Messiah (1:26, 27, 33). The next day, John, like a true minister of the Gospel points his hearers away from himself to Jesus, saying "Behold the Lamb of God which taketh away the sin of the world." He then reveals one of his reasons for baptizing the Lord; namely, that he might have a revelation of His deity (v. 33).

There is no jealousy in John the Baptist. The next day he repeats his message and encourages his followers to follow Jesus. One of the two who heard the message was Andrew, the brother of Peter. The other whose name is not mentioned may have been the author of the Gospel, John. Andrew shows the reality of his spiritual experience by leading his brother Peter to the Messiah. Jesus, seeing in this last-named person one who was destined to become the first living stone of His church, gives him the prophetic name of Cephas (1:42). Jesus then calls Philip, who with enthusiasm, testifies to Nathanael that he has found the Messiah, Jesus of Nazareth. Nathanael can hardly believe that the Messiah has come out of the despised Galilean town of Nazareth, but he is quickly convinced by Jesus' supernatural knowledge that He indeed is the King of Israel.

A marriage at Cana gives Jesus an opportunity to manifest His power. His attendance at such a function shows His love for mingling with the people and sanctifying their gatherings with His presence. The joy of this marriage in particular was in danger of being marred and the giver of the feast being disgraced, for the wine had run out. Mary, knowing her Son's miraculous powers, and desiring with natural motherly pride to see Him manifest them, informs Him of the fact that there is no wine, this reminder carrying with it the indirect suggestion that He supply some. Jesus tenderly reminds her that though He has been subject to her until the time of the beginning of His ministry, their relations are now changed (2:4). He is now guided by His heavenly Father, who has timed every event in His life.

The Jews had allowed the spirit of commercialism to violate the sanctity of the temple precincts, for scattered over the Court of the Gentiles, were sellers of sacrificial animals and money-changers. Such a desecration of His Father's house causes Jesus to drive out these merchants from the temple. Since only a prophet or the Messiah himself could cleanse the temple, the leaders ask the Lord to prove His authority by a sign. He gives them the sign of His death and resurrection. His words respecting this sign were later made the basis of a false charge. Matt. 26:61.

Jesus' miracles had gained Him many followers (2:23), but Jesus did not trust a faith that depended merely on signs. One of those who had been impressed by His miracles was a ruler of the Jews named Nicodemus. He begins his conversation with Jesus by acknowledging that He is a teacher come from God. Jesus ignores this compliment and abruptly tells Nicodemus that he must be born again. It seems that Nicodemus was convinced that the kingdom of God that Jesus was proclaiming was about to be ushered in and therefore wished to **join** it. Our Lord therefore explains that he must be **born** into it. Nicodemus, sharing the common Jewish view, believed that the kingdom would come with outward show. Jesus shows him that it comes by the mysterious working of the Spirit in the heart (3:8). Nicodemus believed, together with other Jews, that the kingdom was to be ushered in by the glorious appearing of the Messiah. Jesus taught him that it must be ushered in by the death of the Messiah (3:14).

John the Baptist's disciples, seeing the crowds leaving him and going to Jesus, complain to their master (3:25, 26). John tells them that this is entirely according to God's plan. He was only the friend of the bridegroom; i.e., the one, who according to Jewish custom asks for the hand of the bride and arranges the marriage. His mission was to lead the bridegroom (the Messiah) to the bride (the Jewish nation) (3:29); this done, his mission was ended (3:30).

Chapter 4 records Jesus' interview with a woman of Samaria. Dr. Torrey draws an interesting contrast between her and Nicodemus:

A woman	A man
A Samaritan	A Jew
A prostitute	A teacher of Israel
Came at noon day	Came at night
Confessed Jesus at once	A secret disciple
Brought a whole city to Christ	Brought (?) to Christ

A common need—the Holy Spirit. John 3:5; 4:14: "There is no difference."

Chapter 5 records the beginning of Jesus' conflicts with the Jews respecting His Divine claims. He is criticized for healing a man on the Sabbath day. He defends himself by affirming that God His

Father is associated with Him in the work of healing on the Sabbath (5:17). Because of that fact, and
because He did nothing apart from the Father
(v. 19), He was perfectly justified in healing suffering
humanity on the Sabbath. Jesus then makes some
astounding claims. He claims to be the raiser of the
dead (vv. 21–29); the One having equal honor with
the Father (v. 23); the Judge of all men (vv. 22, 27).
As witnesses to His claims He appeals to John the
Baptist (v. 33); to His works (v. 36); to the Father
(v. 37); to the Scriptures (v. 39); to Moses (v. 46).

The feeding of the multitude recorded in chapter
6 marks the culmination of Christ's popularity. So
convinced are the people that He was the Prophet
they had been so long waiting for, that they attempt
to make Him King. But Jesus refuses this honor for
He has come not to reign but to die. In the discourse
following this incident (vv. 26, 65), Jesus strikes a
death blow at His popularity, for while they believe
that their salvation is to be brought about by a
glorious Messiah, He teaches them that it was to be
effected by a dying Messiah. He first of all rebukes
them for seeking for the natural food instead of
the spiritual (vv. 26, 27). On their asking Him what
they were to **do** in order to obtain this true food,
He replies that they were to **believe** in Him (vv. 28,
29). The people then ask for a sign in order that they
might believe Him (v. 30), and they mention the
fact that Moses gave them the manna from heaven
(v. 31). Our Lord tells them that the manna was
simply a type of himself, the true Manna (vv. 32, 33,
35). He tells them that as Israel rejected the earthly
manna so they have rejected the heavenly (v. 36). But
though the nation at large has rejected Him, there is
a faithful remnant that will come to Him (v. 37), and
these He will not cast out, for it is His Father's will
to give them everlasting life (vv. 38–40). The Jews
murmur that the Son of a carpenter should claim to

come down from heaven (v. 42). Jesus tells them that a divine revelation is necessary to convince them of His deity (vv. 44, 45). He then shows how they may obtain eternal life—by eating His flesh and drinking His blood; i.e., by believing in Him as the atonement for their sins. The Jews do not understand this figurative language; they take it literally (vv. 52, 60). Jesus then tells them that His words are to be taken not literally, but spiritually (v. 63).

Notice the result of this discourse—a sifting of Jesus' disciples (vv. 60–71).

CHAPTER VI

JOHN 7 TO 12

III. Rejection of Christ's Claims. Chaps 7:1 to 12:50

1. Jesus at the Feast of Tabernacles (Chap. 7)
2. The woman taken in adultery (8:1–11)
3. Discourses on the Light of the World, and spiritual freedom (8:12–59)
4. The healing of the man born blind (Chap. 9)
5. The discourse on the Good Shepherd (10:1–21)
6. Jesus at the Feast of the Dedication (10:22–42)
7. The raising of Lazarus (11:1–46)
8. The final rejection of Christ by the nation (11:47 to 12:50)

The brethren of Jesus urge Him to attend the Feast of Tabernacles in Jerusalem and manifest His works before the people; for they reason that if He really is the Messiah, He ought to make a public proclamation of His claims instead of lingering in an obscure Galilean town (7:1–5). As yet they did not believe His claims, although the time came when they did. Acts 1:14. Jesus replies that the hour for His going to Jerusalem had not yet come. He later goes to the feast in secret (7:10), in order to avoid the caravans of Galilean pilgrims who would recognize Him and perhaps make a public demonstration.

As Jesus begins teaching in the temple, the people are astonished at His preaching, for they know that He had not passed through their theological schools (7:15). Jesus explains that His teaching comes directly from God (v. 16), and if anyone be really willing to do God's will he will find that His teaching is true. Jesus then defends His sincerity, showing that He is not seeking His own glory (v. 18). Looking into the hearts of the people, He sees their hatred for Him, and accuses them of the violation of Moses' law (v. 19). He then defends His action in healing the man on the Sabbath day (vv. 21–24; compare Chap. 5). Seeing Jesus speaking so boldly, some of the people wonder whether the rulers have accepted Him (v. 26). Others cannot believe that He is the Messiah for they know the place of His residence and parents (v. 27). Jesus acknowledges that they know these things, but He tells them that they are ignorant of the fact that He was sent by God (v. 28). Some of the people, remembering Jesus' miracles, are inclined to believe that He is the Messiah (v. 31). The Pharisees hearing this, send officers to arrest Him (v. 32). Whereupon Jesus tells them that their desire to get rid of Him will shortly be gratified (v. 33); but that the time will come when they will seek a Deliverer and will not find any (v. 34). During the Feast of Tabernacles, it was customary for the priests to go to the Pool of Siloam and draw water in a golden pitcher, at the same time chanting Isaiah 12. The water was then poured out upon the altar. This was considered commemorative of the water given in the wilderness, and typical of the future outpouring of the Spirit upon Israel. It was probably at this point that Jesus arose and proclaimed himself the Fountain of living waters, the Rock smitten that the whole world might drink (vv. 37–39). On hearing this claim many people acknowledged that He was the Messiah (v. 40), but others objected that He could not be He for He came from Galilee. The officers of the temple, impressed and awed by Jesus' majestic utterances, do not arrest Him (v. 46). The Pharisees rebuke them, saying that none of the rulers had believed on Him, but only the ignorant people (vv. 47–50). At this point Nicodemus defends the

Lord, whereupon the Pharisees angrily affirm that according to the Scriptures, no prophet came out of Galilee (7:52). This was untrue for both Jonah and Elijah were from that region.

The scribes and Pharisees bring before Jesus a woman caught in adultery and ask Jesus whether or not she should be visited with the penalty laid down in Moses' law. This was an attempt to involve the Lord in a dilemma. If He ruled that the woman should be freed it would be a contradiction of His statement that He had not come to destroy, but to fulfill the law of Moses. Matt. 5:17. If He ruled that the woman should be stoned according to the law, it might be considered a contradiction of His statement that He had come not to judge, but to save sinners. Our Lord settles this question by transferring the case to the court of their conscience. At that court, His questioners found out that "all have sinned and come short of the glory of God."

Jesus then proclaims himself the Light of the world—a claim truly Divine (8:12). The Pharisees object that His own testimony does not prove the truth of His claims (v. 13). Jesus answers that He is able to bear witness of himself for He has a perfect consciousness of His Divine origin and nature (v. 14). He then refers them to His Father's testimony (v. 18); i.e., to the miracles by which God had confirmed His Son's word. Jesus then accuses the Pharisees of ignorance of the Father (v. 19). Though they reject Him, the day will come when they will seek a Messiah (v. 21), but will not find one. He tells them that after His crucifixion and resurrection, when the Spirit should have been outpoured and mighty works wrought in His name—then they would have abundant evidence of His deity (v. 28).

These sayings caused many of the people to believe on Him (8:30), but Jesus, seeing the weakness of their faith exhorts them to continue in His teaching, which teaching would set them completely free from sin (vv. 31, 32). Some of the disciples take offense at this saying, for as Jews, they considered themselves free men (v. 33). Jesus explains that the servitude He referred to was the servitude of sin (vv. 34–37). He then shows that they were not Abraham's seed, because they did not perform Abraham's works; namely, the work of faith (vv. 37–40). He proves the falsity of their claim to be the children of God, by showing them they have rejected God's representative (v. 42). He tells them that their repugnance to the truth and the hatred in their hearts show them to be the children of the devil (v. 44). He challenges them to either convict Him of sin or believe His claims (v. 46). On His promise of exemption from spiritual death to those who believe on Him, He is accused of exalting himself above Abraham (v. 53). Jesus tells them that Abraham foresaw His coming (v. 56). This statement astonishes the Jews who cannot understand how He and Abraham could ever have met (v. 57). Jesus then affirms His preexistence (v. 58). The Jews understand this to be a claim to deity, and attempt to stone Him as a blasphemer (v. 59).

Jesus' healing of a blind man on the Sabbath day again draws upon Him the hatred of the leaders. After an attempt to prove Jesus a sinner, they are confounded by the arguments of the poor, unlettered man who had been healed (Chap. 9).

Possibly to draw a contrast between the false shepherds who had cast out the healed man from the synagogue (9:34), and the true shepherds, Jesus utters the discourse recorded in 10:1–21. Read Ezekiel Chap. 34 in this connection. In verses 1, 2, He has reference to true pastors, who enter the fold through himself the door; meaning those who have a Divine call. In verses 8, 9, 12, Jesus evidently refers to false messiahs and prophets who had misled the people and caused their destruction.

At the Feast of the Dedication, the Jews come to Jesus asking Him whether He is the Christ (10:23, 24). Jesus tells them that His works and words have proved Him to be the Christ (v. 25), but they have not believed for they are not His sheep; they have not obeyed the voice of the Divine Shepherd (vv. 26, 27). Jesus then describes the security of His sheep, and concludes with a claim of oneness with God (v. 30). The Jews attempt to stone Him for claiming to be equal with God. Jesus vindicates His right to call himself the Son of God by an Old Testament reference. He maintains that in those days rulers and judges were sometimes referred to as gods (vv. 34, 35; Ps. 82:6). Therefore if unjust judges, who were temporary representatives of God were called gods, why should not He who was the righteous and eternal Judge call himself the Son of God (v. 36)? He tells them that they need not believe Him if His works are not divine (vv. 37, 38).

The sensation caused by the raising of Lazarus (Chap. 11) brings the priests and Pharisees together in council for the purpose of plotting Jesus' death (11:47). Caiaphas wishes to put Jesus out of the way for political reasons. He argues that if Jesus is allowed to continue His ministry, His popularity will cause a popular tumult which will excite the suspicion of the Romans, and which will result in the loss of power and office on the part of the rulers, and calamity on the part of the nation. He therefore reasons that it is better for one man to suffer, rather than the whole nation (vv. 49, 50). This is what He meant by His words in verse 50. But God meant them as a prophecy of the atoning death of the Messiah (vv. 51, 52).

Chapter 12 records two events mentioned by the other Evangelists: the anointing of Jesus, and the triumphal entry. During the Feast of the Passover, a request of some Gentiles to see Him (12:20) calls forth a prophecy of His death which was to bring salvation to the Gentile world (v. 24). He then marks out the path which His disciples must follow—that of self-denial and even death (vv. 25, 26). Though the thought of a shameful death is utterly repulsive to Him, yet He does not shrink from it (v. 27). He announces His death to be the judgment of the world (v. 31), the defeat of Satan (v. 31), and the means of attracting sin-sick humanity (v. 32). Chapter 12:37–41 records the general result of Christ's ministry to Israel—rejection of the light followed by spiritual blindness on their part. The remaining verses of this chapter contain Jesus' last appeal to the nation.

CHAPTER VII

JOHN 13 TO 21

IV. Christ's Manifestation to His Disciples
(Chaps. 13–17)

1. Farewell discourses (Chaps. 13–17)
2. Intercessory prayer (Chap. 17)

Chapter 13:1–17 contains the supreme example of Christ's humility. With full knowledge of His deity (v. 3), He stoops to the most menial of tasks, the washing of His disciples' feet. The reason for this act is explained by Him (vv. 13–17); it was done in part as an example to His followers that they should humble themselves and serve one another. And they needed that lesson. (See Luke 22:24.)

There is room for much doubt whether our Lord intended to establish an ordinance of literal foot-washing for all time, particularly since it was the custom of the day for the host to provide water and towel, with a servant to wash his guests' feet, in view of the fact that open sandals were worn and naturally the feet would become soiled by the journey over the dirty street or dusty road.

A much deeper meaning seems to lie here, because what Christ did was altogether in view of His cross and His subsequent session as our High Priest and Advocate at the Father's right hand. "When Jesus knew that His hour was come that He should depart out of this world unto the Father (v. 1), knowing that the Father had given all things into His hands, and that He was come from God and went to God; He riseth from supper and laid aside His garments and took a towel and girded himself" (vv. 3, 4).

The context here, then, clearly shows that what He did was a type of His future redemptive and priestly work. We take it that He here enacted symbolically this ministry of His to keep clean the feet (the daily walk) of His saints. "If any man sin, we have an advocate with the Father, Jesus Christ the righteous." 1 John 2:1.

He says to Peter, "What I do **thou knowest not now**, but thou **shalt know hereafter**." Peter surely knew that Christ was about literally to wash his feet, but the Lord indicates that the meaning of this act, he would not understand till later in his experience. Peter, after his terrible lapse in denying Christ, knew then what Christ's words, "I have prayed for you that your faith fail not," really meant, when he was cleansed and restored to fellowship with his Lord.

After the announcement of His betrayal, and the exit of the betrayer, Jesus reveals the spirit that is to characterize the relations of His disciples to one another during His absence; namely, love (v. 34). This fact that they love one another is to be the badge of Christian discipleship (v. 35).

After hearing about the Lord's coming death and departure, the disciples are saddened. It is then that He speaks the comforting words mentioned in chapter 14. As a cure for their troubled condition, He suggests three things: that they have faith in Him (v. 1); the fact that He is going to prepare a place for them (v. 2); the fact that He is coming again (v. 3). In reply to Thomas' question as to the way to heaven (v. 5), He replies that He himself is the way. He is the way because He is the image and the Revealer of the Father (vv. 7, 9). His complete union with the Father is shown by the fact that even the words He spoke and the works He wrought were through the direct power of the Father. And such was to be their union with Him that the disciples were to perform the same works

(v. 12). This was to be accomplished through prayer (v. 13). Obedience to His commandments and love toward Him would result in His sending to them the Comforter, who was now dwelling **with**, but who would later be **in** them (vv. 16, 17); it would also result in the Father and the Son manifesting Themselves to them (vv. 21–25). In verse 26 He explains the ministry of the Spirit in relation to the disciples. He makes His last legacy to His disciples—His peace (vv. 27, 28).

In the next chapter Jesus explains the relation of the disciples to Him during His absence—a vital, organic union typified by a vine and its branches. He shows how this true vine is kept clean and fruitful; namely by taking away unfruitful branches, and purging the sound branches (v. 2). They have already been purged by His teaching (v. 3), but He exhorts them to abide in Him in order to maintain this vital union (vv. 4–6). He shows them how their prayers may be answered; by abiding in Him, and His words abiding in them (v. 7). If they bear fruit two results will follow: the Father will be glorified, and they will prove themselves to be true disciples (v. 8). He exhorts them to continue in His love (v. 9), this to be accomplished by keeping His commandments (v. 10). Unity among themselves is to be maintained by the spirit of love (vv. 12, 13). By keeping His commandments, they come into a closer relationship with Him—that of friends (v. 15). Contrary to the usual order, He, the teacher has chosen them His disciples (v. 16). He has chosen them for a specific purpose—that of bearing fruit and enjoying a peculiar fellowship in prayer with the Father (v. 16). The remaining verses of Chapter 15 reveal the attitude of the world toward the disciples.

In order that they may not be thrown into consternation and discouragement when persecutions arise, He tells them what to expect from the

world (Chap. 16:1–4). They are sad at His leaving
them, but it is necessary that He go in order that
the Comforter might come (v. 7). For while He is
in the flesh, He can be present only in one place at
a time, but seated at the right hand of the Father
and sending forth the Spirit, He can be present
with every one of His followers, "even unto the
end of the age." He then explains the threefold
ministry of the Spirit in relation to the world: He
will convict the world of the fact that unbelief in
Him is a sin; He will reveal the fact that He, the
Crucified, is the righteous One; though the evil
may prosper and the righteous suffer, He will
convince the world that there is a judgment to
come that will set things right (vv. 8–12). He then
explains the ministry of the Comforter in relation
to the disciples (vv. 12–15). Jesus tells them that
His departure in death will make them sad but
that they will see Him again and their mourning
will be turned to rejoicing (vv. 16–22). They would
see Him again first after His resurrection; second,
with the eye of faith; and finally, face to face. After
His ascension, it would not be necessary to make
their requests to Him (v. 23), neither would it be
necessary for Him to ask on their behalf (v. 26),
for they would have direct access to the Father
(vv. 23, 27).

Chapter 17 records the great high priestly
prayer of Jesus. We give a simple outline of this
prayer:

   I. Prayer for himself (vv. 1–5)
     1. For His own glorification.
  II. Prayer for His disciples (vv. 6–19)
     1. For preservation (v. 11)
     2. For sanctification (v. 17)
 III. Prayer for all believers (vv. 20–26)
     1. For unity (vv. 21, 22)
     2. For their presence with Him (vv. 24)

V. Christ's Humiliation and Glorification
(Chaps. 18–21)

1. The betrayal and arrest (18:1–18)
2. The trial before Caiaphas and Pilate (18:19 to 19:16)
3. The crucifixion (19:17–42)
4. The resurrection (20:1–10)
5. The appearances of Jesus to His disciples (20:10 to 21:25)

Jesus is first brought before Annas, the father-in-law of Caiaphas for a preliminary hearing (18:19–23). He is questioned as to His doctrine because they believed that He had been spreading dangerous secret teachings. Jesus defends himself by asserting that all His teaching has been done openly and in public (vv. 20, 21). He is then sent to the high priest for the formal trial, which is described by the other writers.

After His condemnation for blasphemy (Matt. 26:65), Jesus is led to Pilate for the execution of the sentence. The Jews evidently hope that Pilate will ratify their sentence without asking questions, but he is in no mood to gratify the desire of the priests whom he heartily despised. He tells them to judge Him according to their law; he does not care to judge religious cases (v. 31). But since the power of inflicting capital punishment had been taken away from the Jews years before, they could not now execute the sentence of death (v. 31). Jesus had been accused of declaring himself king. Luke 23:2. This was a serious offense in the eyes of the Romans. Pilate therefore questions Jesus concerning His kingdom (vv. 33–35). Our Lord makes it clear that His kingdom is a spiritual one, not a temporal one (v. 36) and that the members of His kingdom are those whose hearts are open to the truth (v. 37). Pilate makes several attempts to release Jesus, but the determination of the Jews to crucify Him, is stronger than his determination to release Him, and upon the Jews' threatening to report him to the emperor, he yields (19:12, 13).

John, in his account of the crucifixion, mentions some details additional to those found in the other Gospels; namely, Pilate's writing of the accusation (vv. 19–22); the parting of Jesus' garments (vv. 23, 24), the committing of His mother to John (vv. 26, 27), the two utterances on the cross (vv. 28, 30) and the piercing of Jesus' side. Sometimes the bones of crucified criminals were broken in order to hasten death. In Jesus' case this was not necessary for He was already dead. A fulfillment of prophecy was involved in this incident (vv. 36, 37). The fact that Jesus had died so soon, seems to show that it was spiritual sufferings and not physical, that caused His death, for persons crucified usually lingered for about three days (See Mark 15:44). Physicians tell us that the water and blood issuing from Jesus' side indicated a broken heart.

Note how John, in his description of the empty tomb is careful to mention sufficient details to refute the false report that the disciples had stolen Jesus' body. Matt. 28:11–15.

We shall notice here the appearances of Jesus after His resurrection.

1. To Mary Magdalene. 20:11–18.

2. To the apostles, Thomas being absent (20:19–23). In order to convince the fearful and unbelieving disciples of the reality of His resurrection, Jesus shows them His wounds. He then gives them their commission (v. 21), their equipment (prophetically and symbolically, v. 22), and their authority (v. 23). Note that the last mentioned verse refers to church discipline. (Compare Matt. 18:15–18.)

3. To the Apostles, Thomas being present (vv. 24–29). Though loyal in character (11–16), Thomas is

skeptical. He will not believe until he sees. His unbelief had evidently delayed the disciples' going into Galilee. Matt. 28:7. Though a sceptic, Thomas' heart is honest; he wants to know the truth. Jesus meets his desire, and Thomas becomes as intensely believing as he was once unbelieving.

4. To the Seven at the Sea of Galilee (Chap. 21). After the miraculous draught of fishes and the meal, Jesus gives Peter his commission as shepherd of His sheep. The thrice-repeated question may refer to Peter's three denials. Verses 20–24 of the same chapter were written by John to correct a false impression that had been produced among the disciples by Jesus' words to Peter (v. 22). It was believed that Jesus meant that John should not die (v. 23). John shows those words did not mean that he should not die, but that, **if** Jesus willed that John should tarry till He comes, it was none of Peter's concern.

CHAPTER VIII

ACTS 1 TO 5

Theme. The book of Acts gives the history of the establishment and growth of the Christian church, and of the proclaiming of the Gospel to the then known world according to Christ's command and by the power of His Spirit. It is a record of Christ's ministry as it was continued through His servants. Leon Tucker suggests the following key words: Ascension, Descension, Extension. The ascension of Christ is followed by the descension of the Spirit, and the descension of the Spirit is followed by the extension of the Gospel.

Author. Luke. As we consider the dedication of the book to Theophilus (Acts 1:1; compare Luke 1:3), the reference to a former treatise (Acts 1:1), its style, the fact that the author was a companion of Paul as shown by the fact that portions of the book are written in the first person (16:10), and that this companion accompanied Paul to Rome (27:1; compare Col. 4:14; Philemon 24; 2 Tim. 4:11), we conclude that the Acts was written by Luke. Ancient writers bear out this fact.

To Whom Written. It was written in particular to Theophilus, a Christian gentleman, but in general for the whole church.

Contents

I. The Church of Jerusalem (Chaps 1:1 to 8:4)

1. Introductory chapter (Chap. 1)
2. The outpouring of the Spirit (2:1–13)
3. Peter's sermon and its results (2:14–47)
4. The healing of the lame man, and Peter's sermon (3:1–26)
5. Peter and John before the council (4:1–22)
6. The first prayer meeting (4:23–31)
7. The consecration of the early church (4:32–37)
8. The sin of Ananias and Sapphira (5:1–16)
9. The arrest of Peter and John (5:17–42)
10. The first church difficulty and its settlement (6:1–7)
11. The ministry of Stephen (6:8–15)
12. Stephen's discourse before the council (Chap. 7)
13. The first persecution of the church (8:1–4)

The book of Acts really begins at chapter 2, which describes the outpouring of the Spirit and the commencement of the Church. Chapter 1 is simply introductory and describes events leading up to the great event of the Day of Pentecost.

To what writing does the author refer in 1:1? What does he say concerning Jesus in the same verse? Which is mentioned first, "do" or "teach"? When did Jesus give commands unto the apostles through the Spirit (v. 2; compare Matt. 28:16–20; Mark 16:14–20; Luke 24:44–53; John 20:19–23)? Mention one of the "infallible proofs" (v. 3) of Christ's resurrection. Luke 24:39–43. What command was then given (v. 4)? When did the Father promise the Holy Spirit? Joel 2:28. When did Jesus promise Him? John. 14:16–17; 15:26; 16:7–15. Did Jesus mention the exact day on which the Spirit would be outpoured (v. 5)? Why not? (Compare Mark 13:37.) What question did the disciples ask at this time (v. 6)? Had the kingdom been taken from Israel? Matt. 21:43. Did Jesus answer this question directly? Will the kingdom ever be restored to Israel? Rom. 11:25–27. When? Matt. 23:39; Luke 21:24; Rom. 11:25; Acts 3:19–20; Zech. 12:10. What must take place before that event? Acts 1:8; 15:14; Rom. 11:25. Where was the ministry of the apostles to begin and end (1:8)? In what city does the book of Acts begin? In what city does it end? What Old Testament scripture should be quoted with the last-named verse? Zech. 4:6. What happened after Jesus had given His commands to the apostles? From what mountain did Jesus ascend (v. 12)? On what mountain will He descend at His second coming? Zech. 14:4. What company is mentioned in verse 13? Who is mentioned first? Why? What other companies are mentioned in verse 14? Was there a time when Jesus' brethren did not believe on Him? John 7:5. Who was the spokesman of the apostles (v. 15)? How many disciples were gathered at that time? What Old Testament Scriptures does Peter quote in relation to Judas? Ps. 69:25; 109:8.

Chapter 1:18 seems to contradict Matt. 27:5, but the logical inference from a comparison of the two verses is that Judas hanged himself and then fell to earth. A true incident is recorded of a man who committed suicide by sitting on the window sill in the fourth story of a house and then shooting himself. One writer might have described the whole event; another might have recorded only the shooting; another might have mentioned just the fact of his fall from the window. All three would have been right.

Why was Peter anxious that the complete number of the apostles should be made up? Matt. 19:28; Rev. 21:14. What two qualifications were necessary for an apostle (vv. 21, 23)?

The two qualifications necessary for an apostle were first, that he should have walked with the Lord during His earthly ministry; second, that he should have seen Him after His resurrection. The question has often been raised whether or not Matthias was divinely appointed as an apostle or whether Paul is the twelfth apostle. It is the writer's opinion that Matthias was the twelfth apostle. Though Paul was an apostle who had seen the Lord, and had been divinely appointed to his office, he did not possess the first qualification—that of having walked with the Lord during His earthly ministry. He did not bear that peculiar relation to Jesus that the Twelve did. (See John 15:27.)

We now come to the events of the Day of Pentecost. The death and resurrection of Christ, and the outpouring of the Spirit represent the fulfilling of the types of three feasts which followed one another in succession; namely, Passover, (Lev. 23:5), the Feast of the First-fruits (Lev. 23:10–14), and the Feast of Pentecost (Lev. 23:15–21). The Passover was typical of Christ's atoning death. Following the Passover, was the Feast of the First-fruits, on which feast the first-fruits of the harvest were waved before the Lord. This ceremony was typical of Christ's resurrection as "the first-fruits" from the dead. From this feast fifty days were counted, and on the last day the Feast of Pentecost was celebrated (hence the name "Pentecost," meaning fifty). On this feast two loaves—the first loaves of the wheat harvest—were waved before the Lord, this being typical of the consecration of the first members of the church.

Did the Holy Spirit inspire and empower people in Old Testament times? Num. 11:26; 1 Sam. 10:6; Ps. 51:11; Mic. 3:8. Were people **filled** with the Spirit before Christ died? Luke 1:15, 41, 67. Compare John 7:39. What then was the difference between the imparting of the Spirit in those days and that in New Testament times? We will answer this question.

1. In Old Testament times the Spirit was given to only a few—to persons in some particular office, as prophet, priest or judge. Now He is poured out upon **all flesh**. Joel 2:28.

2. In those days the impartation of the Spirit was **temporary;** now He abides with us **forever**.

It is interesting to note that for every manifestation of the Spirit mentioned in the New Testament, a counterpart may be found in the Old, except for one—the speaking in other tongues. The inference drawn from this fact is that the speaking in other tongues is the manifestation of the Spirit that is intended to be peculiar to this dispensation.

What three manifestations accompanied the outpouring of the Spirit? Was the speaking in other tongues simply for the purpose of preaching the Gospel to every one in his own language (2:8–11, compare 10:46)? Note that those receiving the Baptism do not always speak in a known tongue but generally in an unknown tongue. (Compare 1 Cor. Chap. 14.) In this instance known tongues were spoken, because since this was the first manifestation of this kind, it was necessary to convince the unbelieving Jews that this was a genuine manifestation of the Spirit, and not mere gibberish, as some might have supposed.

What two effects did this manifestation produce on the hearers (vv. 12, 13)? In what sense were the disciples drunk? Eph. 5:18. Note how Peter defended them against the charge of being drunk. The Jews did not generally eat or drink before the hour of prayer which came about 9 AM. How did Peter explain this manifestation (2:16–21)? Did Joel's prophecy find its **complete** fulfillment at this time? When will it be completely fulfilled in relation to Israel? Zech. 12:10. Who, in Old Testament times, prayed for this event? Num. 11:29. In his sermon, does Peter declare immediately that Jesus is the Messiah (v. 22,

compare v. 36)? What does he do first? What first
proof does he offer of Christ's Messiahship (v. 22)?
What second proof (v. 24)? What third proof (v. 33)?
What was the effect of this sermon? What did Peter
tell the Jews to do (v. 38)? What two things would
follow their repentance (v. 38)? What else did he
tell them to do besides repenting (v. 40)? What can
you say concerning the unity of the first Christians
(vv. 44–47)? What was the outward manifestation
of their unity (v. 45)? Do you believe that they were
commanded to have all things in common, or was
this act spontaneous, born of Spirit-inspired love for
the brethren? Are we, under the conditions in which
we now live, to follow literally their example, or are
we to manifest the same Spirit?

Chapter 3 records the first apostolic miracle.
Notice its characteristics. It was performed upon a
man whose infirmity was incurable, and it was performed openly so it could be verified by all.

Were the actions of the healed man in the temple
very dignified? In New Testament times, when
people wanted or received something from the Lord
God, did they always consult their dignity? Luke
17:15; 19:3, 4. From whom did Peter point the people
(3:12)? To whom did he point them (v. 13)? What
contrast does he draw between God's treatment of
Christ and their treatment (vv. 13–15)? As what kind
of person did the Jews consider Jesus? Matt. 26:65;
John 9:24. What did Peter say had been done in His
name (v. 16)? What was the logical conclusion from
this fact, as to Jesus' character? John 9:33. Did the
Jews have some excuse for their action in crucifying
Christ (v. 17)? Was this ignorance entirely excusable?
John 12:37, 38. Who was a type of the Jewish nation
in this respect? 1 Tim. 1:13. Was the Jewish nation
rejected because they crucified Christ, the Son, or
because they rejected the **Spirit**, who testified of His
resurrection and exaltation? Compare Acts 13:46.

What appeal did Peter make to the nation (v. 19)? What does he say will follow their repentance as a nation (vv. 19, 20)? Will they ever repent? Zech. 12:10; Matt. 23:39; Rom. 11:26. What is meant by "the restitution of all things" promised by, the **prophets?** Isaiah Chap. 11; Jer. 23:5, 6; Amos 9:11–15; Zech. 14:16–21. Did the prophets ever predict the final restitution of the wicked and of the devil and his angels? To which prophets does Peter refer them? Why should they be the first to believe the prophets (v. 25)? What privilege was Israel's (v. 26; compare Matt. 15:24; Acts 13:46; Rom. 1:16; Rom. 15:8)?

Chapter 4 records the first persecution of the apostles on the part of religious authorities.

What was the central theme of the apostles' preaching (v. 2)? Why did this grieve the Sadducees? Matt. 22:23. What was the result of Peter's last sermon (v. 4)? What explains the boldness of an uneducated fisherman in the presence of the religious leaders (v. 8)? Of what did Peter accuse them (v. 10)? To what Old Testament Scripture did he refer them (v. 11, compare Ps. 118:22)? Where did Peter probably learn this Scripture together with its meaning and application? Matt. 21:42. What warning did he utter to them (v. 12)? Whose image did the priests see in Peter and John (v. 13)? Why could they not take action against the apostles (v. 14)? What admission did they make (v. 16)? What should this admission have led them to do? When did the same people make a similar admission? John 11:47. Did their attempt to intimidate the apostles succeed (vv. 19, 20)? What was the effect of this miracle on the people (v. 21)?

What did the opposition of the leaders lead the disciples to do (4:24)? What psalm did they quote in their prayer (vv. 25, 26; see Psalm 2)? What three petitions did they make (vv. 29, 30)? How long was it before the answer came? What three things happened (v. 31)?

What can you say concerning the consecration of the early church (4:32–37)? Who is mentioned at this point as an example of a consecrated Christian (v. 36)? Who wanted to have the same honor without paying the same price (5:1)? What was probably at the bottom of their sin? 1 Tim. 6:10. What sin did it lead to? Luke 12:1. In what sin did it finally culminate? What was the penalty of their sin? Does God always punish similar offenders in this way, or did He punish these two as an example to others, and to show that the Church was a holy institution where no deceit would be tolerated? What was the effect of this judgment on the Church (5:11)? On the people (v. 13)? Would hypocrites care to join such a church? What promise of the Lord found its fulfillment in 5:15, 16? John 14:12.

What effect did the ministry of Peter have on the Sadducees (5:17)? How did they try to hinder the Word of life? What did God have to say in the matter (5:20)? What was making the Sadducees uneasy (v. 28)? Was the blood of the Lord really upon them? John 11:47–53. Did Peter tell them that Jesus' blood was upon them (vv. 30, 31)? What two witnesses to Jesus' resurrection did Peter cite (v. 32)? Who showed more wisdom than the other leaders (v. 34)? Who was his distinguished pupil (22:3)? Was his advice wise as far as natural wisdom was concerned?

In the above incident, Dr. Griffith-Thomas notices three representative forces—the spirit of error (the Sadducees); the spirit of compromise (Gamaliel); the spirit of truth (Peter).

CHAPTER IX
ACTS 6:1 TO 12:23

Chapter 6 records the first church difficulty and its solution. Notice that this difficulty was unavoidable because the organization of the church had not increased in proportion to its growth (v. 1). Notice also that it was serious, for it threatened a division in the church between those Jews brought up in Palestine (Hebrews) and those who had received a Greek education, or who had lived in Greek-speaking countries (Grecians). This difficulty was settled in the spirit of love and cooperation, and found its solution in increased organization—the instituting of a new order in the church ministry (deacons).

To what ministry did the apostles wish to limit themselves (6:4)? What three qualifications for a deacon are mentioned here (v. 3)? Note that though it is not recorded that these were called deacons, their ministry shows them to be such (deacon comes from a Greek word meaning servant). Who was the most distinguished of all these deacons? How did the Lord witness to His pleasure at the amiable settlement of the difficulty (v. 7)? Is it necessary for one to be an apostle in order to work miracles (v. 8)? With whom did Stephen dispute? Why were they not able to resist his arguments and preaching (v. 10, Luke 21:15)? Verbal arguments failing, to what did they resort (vv. 11–14)? What was the charge against him? Did he look like a blasphemer (v. 15)? In his defense, Stephen reviews Israel's history from Abraham to Solomon. Running through his discourse are the following thoughts:

1. Divine revelation is progressive. Stephen had been accused of preaching that the law of Moses would pass away (v. 14). Though his words had been misquoted and their meaning perverted, Stephen had evidently been preaching the passing of the age of law, and the ushering in of the age of grace. So he shows that God has always been giving new revelations of himself. First He revealed himself to Abraham, through the institution of the altar; to Moses in the burning bush and on Mount Sinai; then to Israel, through the tabernacle, and finally through the temple. Stephen shows that God's dwelling in the tabernacle and temple was only symbolical (vv. 48, 49). God now dwells in and reveals himself in reality through a new institution—the Church.

2. He had been accused of declaring that the temple would be destroyed (6:14). He shows that the temple is not the only holy place, but that God reveals himself anywhere He finds an open heart. He revealed himself to Abraham in Mesopotamia (v. 2); to Joseph in Egypt (vv. 9–12); to Moses in Egypt (v. 25), and in the wilderness (vv. 30–33, 38).

3. Israel has always rejected God's first offer of mercy, suffered for it, and then has accepted it the second time. They rejected Joseph and Moses the first time, but accepted them the second time (vv. 9–13, 24–35). In like manner they have rejected Jesus, but after they have suffered, they will accept His second offer.

With what two charges against the Jewish leaders did Stephen conclude his discourse (vv. 51, 52)? What Old Testament Scriptures bear out these charges? Isa. 63:10; 2 Chron. 36:15, 16; Neh. 9:30. Did Jesus bring a similar accusation against them? Matt. 5:12; 23:34–39. Who were the real breakers of the law (v. 53)? What vision did Stephen behold (vv. 55, 56)? What did he say? Who had uttered similar words before the same council? Matt. 26:64. What were Stephen's last two utterances (vv. 59, 60)? Who spoke similar words on a like occasion? Luke 23:34, 46. Who is mentioned at this point? Was Stephen's prayer for his slayers answered in this young man? (Compare 1 Tim. 1:13.)

Chapter 8:1–4 records the first general persecution against the whole church. Saul appears here as the most active agent in this persecution. Borne along by his characteristic zeal and energy, he became the champion of Judaism against what he believed to be the heresy of Christianity. What did Saul think he was doing in persecuting the Christians? John 16:2. What was his moral and religious character? Phil. 3:5, 6. In spite of his morality, zeal and sincerity, what was he while he was persecuting the Christians? 1 Tim. 1:13. Did God ever forgive him? Did Paul ever forgive himself? 1 Cor. 15:9. Did this persecution hinder or advance the work of the Lord (8:4; 11:19–21)?

II. The Transition Period: the Church of Palestine and Syria. Chaps. 8:5 to 12:23.

1. The Gospel in Samaria. 8:5–25.
2. The Ethiopian eunuch. 8:26–40.
3. The conversion of Saul. 9:1–22.
4. Saul's ministry in Jerusalem and flight to Tarsus. 9:23–31.
5. Peter's ministry in Lydda and Joppa. 9:32–43.
6. Cornelius' vision. 10:1–8.
7. Peter's vision. 10:9–18.
8. The first sermon to the Gentiles. 10:19–48.
9. Peter's defense for his preaching to the Gentiles. 11:1–18.
10. The establishment of the church at Antioch. 11:19–30)
11. Herod's persecution of the church. Chap. 12.

Who is the Philip mentioned in 8:5 (21:8)? Who had first sown the seed in Samaria (John, Chap. 4)?

What did Philip preach (v. 5)? With whom does he stand in contrast in this respect (v. 9)? What accompanied Philip's preaching (vv. 6, 7)? What was the general effect of this great revival (v. 8)? Was Simon really converted? (Compare vv. 21–23.) What kind of faith was his? (Compare John 2:23, 24.) What motive evidently was at the root of his following Philip (vv. 18, 19)? Had Simon seen manifestations of the Spirit's power (vv. 6, 7)? Had he seen joy (v. 8)? What was there in the Baptism of the Spirit that impressed him (vv. 18, 19)? Did Simon manifest true repentance (v. 24)? Was he really sorry for his sin, or was he afraid of what might happen to him?

Where was Philip told to go (8:26)? Why was it necessary that he leave the scene of a great revival to go to a desert? Was any one else willing to go out of his way to speak to one soul? John, Chap. 4. By whom was Philip led (v. 29)? What very important question did he put to the eunuch (v. 30)? Of what did the man feel the need? How has Jesus supplied this need? John 16:13; Luke 24:45. What passage of Scripture was the eunuch reading? What could he not understand (v. 34)? On what condition did Philip baptize the eunuch (v. 37)? What mode of rapid transportation was used here (v. 39)? Of what is that typical? 1 Thess. 4:17.

Had Saul's hatred for the Christians abated (9:1–4)? To what city was he about to extend his activities? Where was he when he saw the Lord? Whom did Jesus say that Saul was persecuting? What does this teach concerning the believers' relation to the Lord? Matt. 10:40.

"It is hard for thee to kick against the pricks [or goads]." In the East, when an animal became stubborn, the driver would prod it with an iron-pointed rod. The animal's movements then would increase the pain. Jesus wished to teach Paul that he was fighting against God, and that in so doing he was but hurting himself.

How long was it before Saul repented (v. 6)? How did he address Jesus? Did Saul really see the Lord? 1 Cor. 9:1. What could he always claim? Gal. 1:1. Who was now commissioned to minister to Saul? Was the Lord very specific in giving directions (v. 11)? What was Saul's occupation during the three days of his blindness (v. 11)? To what three classes was Saul to preach (v. 15)? What was Jesus to reveal to Saul (v. 16)? What side of the ministry did Jesus always show first to prospective disciples? Luke 14:25–33. Does He show the other side? Matt. 19:28, 29. How did Ananias address Saul (v. 17)? What did Saul receive at this time? What did Paul immediately do (v. 19)?

What happened between verses 22 and 23? Gal. 1:15–17. What was the attitude of the disciples to Paul when he came to Jerusalem (v. 26)? Who befriended him at this time? In what danger was Paul (v. 29)? What vision did he have at this time (22:17, 18)? Where was Paul sent (v. 30)? How long did he stay there (11:25)? About eight years. What was the effect on the church of the removal of its great persecutor (v. 31)?

What was Peter's destination on this journey (9:32, 43)? What events happened during this time? What actions of Peter in raising Tabitha resemble those of the Lord when He raised the ruler's daughter (vv. 40–42; compare Mark 5:40, 41)? What was the effect of Peter's miracles in Lydda and Joppa? What was the main purpose of Peter's visit at Joppa (10:6)?

What three things are said concerning Cornelius' character (10:2)? What was his position? To whom did Jesus prophesy the salvation of the Gentiles? Matt. 8:5–13. Was Cornelius a saved man (11:14)? But what in the condition of his heart made it sure

that God would reveal Christ unto him (vv. 2, 35)?
Had Cornelius been praying along this line (10:31)?
What was he doing when he saw a vision (v. 3)?
Where does God usually meet men? Dan. 9:3, 21;
Acts 22:17, 18. At what hour was Cornelius praying
(Compare 3:1)? Why did not the angels preach the
Gospel to Cornelius instead of telling him where to
find a preacher (vv. 5, 6; 2 Cor. 5:18)? Did angels ever
preach the Gospel? Luke 2:10, 11.

Notice the meaning of Peter's vision. He was
told by a voice from heaven to do something
that was contrary to the Mosaic law (vv. 12–14).
This was symbolical that the dispensation of law
was to pass away. The fact that the command
was repeated signifies that God's purpose was
established. (Compare Gen. 41:32.) The fact that
the sheet was taken up into heaven signifies that
the purpose symbolized by the sheet and animals
was divine.

Did Peter understand at the time the meaning of
the vision (v. 17)? When did he understand (v. 22)?
Whom did Peter take with him (v. 23)? Why (vv. 45,
46; 11:12)? What verse condemns saint worship
of the Roman church (v. 25)? What did Peter say
was the attitude of Jews toward Gentiles (v. 28)?
Did the Old Testament prophesy the salvation of
the Gentiles? Ps. 22:27; Isa. 49:6; Hosea 2:23. Did
Jesus prophesy their salvation? Matt. 8:11; 21:23;
John 10:16. Did the Old Testament ever teach that
the Jew and the Gentile would belong to the **same
body**? Eph. 3:3–6.

What had Peter learned (vv. 34, 35)? What
does verse 38 say concerning Jesus? When was He
anointed? Matt. 3:16. For what purpose? Compare
Luke 4:18. How did Peter know that (v. 39)? What
happened as Peter was speaking? What was the
effect on the Jews who were with Peter? What
proved conclusively to these prejudiced Jews that

the Gentiles had received the Spirit? How were these Gentiles saved (15:9; compare Rom. 10:17)?

What shows the prejudice of the Jews against the Gentiles (11:2, 3)? How did Peter defend himself? How did he show that God put no difference between Jew and Gentile (v. 15)? What were the Jews compelled to admit (v. 18)?

How far did those who had been scattered by Paul's persecution travel (11:19)? To whom did they limit their ministry (v. 20)? To whom did some of them preach? (Note that the word "Grecians" is rendered in some versions "Greeks"; i.e., Gentiles.) What was the spiritual condition of the church at Antioch (v. 23)? Who was sent to preach to them? What three things are said concerning him? Where did he go for help (v. 25)? How long did they remain at Antioch? What characterized the disciples at that time (11:26)? What gift of the Spirit was exercised at this time (v. 28)? What shows the liberality of the church at Antioch (v. 29)?

The Herod mentioned in 12:1 is Herod Agrippa I, the grandson of Herod the Great. Matt. 2:1.

Had James' martyrdom been indirectly prophesied? Matt. 20:22, 23. Why did Herod have Peter arrested? To what did the church have recourse (v. 5)? What happened the last time the church prayed during a crisis (4:31)? What happened this time? Does it look as if those praying really expected an answer to their prayers (v. 15)? What may have been their condition? Luke 24:44. What was God's judgment on Herod?

CHAPTER X

ACTS 12:24 TO 15:35

III. The Church of the Gentiles. Chaps. 12:24 to 21:17
1. Paul's first missionary journey. 12:24 to 14:28.
2. The council at Jerusalem. Chap. 15:1–35.
3. Paul's second missionary journey. Chaps. 15:36 to 18:22.
4. Paul's third missionary journey. Chaps. 18:23 to 21:17.

(In the sections dealing with Paul's journeys, the use of a map is almost a necessity. Let the student so study each journey that he will be able to trace from memory Paul's itinerary, mentioning briefly what occurred at each place.)

Whom did Paul and Barnabas bring from Jerusalem at this time? 12:25. What relation was he to Barnabas? Col. 4:10. What church sent forth Paul and Barnabas? How was this church started (11:19)? Who called these two to their ministry? Is it said that Mark was called also? What may this explain (13:13)? Where does Paul stand in the list of workers at Antioch (13:1)?

1. Paul's first missionary journey. 12:24 to 14:28.

Let us now trace together Barnabas' and Paul's journey step by step. If possible, have a map before you.

Antioch. This was the missionary headquarters of the Church.

Seleucia. This was the seaport of Antioch.

Cyprus. An island in the Mediterranean Sea. The early home of Barnabas (4:36).

Salamis. What did the missionaries do in this town. (13:5)?

Paphos. Who was the first person the missionaries met at this town? What did he attempt to do (13:8)? What struggle is exemplified here? 1 John 4:6; compare 2 Tim. 3:8. By what power did Paul pronounce judgment upon the sorcerer (13:9)? What was the effect of this judgment (v. 12)? What change of name occurs at this point (v. 9)?

Perga. Who has been leader up to this point (13:1; 12:25)? Who assumes the leadership now (13:13)? What happened at this town? How can we explain Mark's action? (Compare 13:2.) Did Mark ever "make good"? 2 Tim. 4:11.

Antioch in Pisidia. The service of the Jewish synagogue consisted usually of prescribed prayers and the reading of the Law and the Prophets. If a preacher or teacher were present, he was called upon to give a message. (Compare Luke 4:16–21.) Paul began his message with a review of Israel's history up to the time of David (vv. 17–25). He then showed that Jesus was of the seed of David (vv. 25–33). He based Jesus' claims as Son of God and Messiah on His resurrection from the dead (vv. 26–37). He then offered the Gospel to the Jews and warned them against rejecting it (vv. 38–41).

Who were particularly anxious to hear the Gospel (v. 42)? How great a hunger for the Word of God was there (v. 44)? What were the feelings of the Jews on seeing the Word of God preached to Gentiles (v. 45)? Of what prophecy was this attitude a fulfillment? Deut. 32:21. What was their attitude toward the Gospel (v. 45)? What did Paul and Barnabas say was necessary (v. 46)? Why? Matt. 10:6; 15:24; John 4:22; Rom. 1:16; 15:8. What did he say that their rejection of the Gospel would mean to the Gentiles (v. 46; compare Rom. 11:11)? Though persecuted by them, what were always

Paul's feelings toward his people? Rom. 9:1–3; 10:1. How did the Gentiles receive the Gospel (v. 48)? Arguments failing, what did the Jews then do? What did Paul and Barnabas do (51)? Was there any command to this effect? Matt. 10:14.

Iconium. What shows that Paul had not yet forsaken his people (14:1)? What were the two results of his preaching in this town (vv. 2, 3)? How did the Lord confirm their preaching (v. 3)? What did their ministry cause in the city (v. 4)? What did they do when they heard of coming persecution (v. 6)? Had they any command to this effect? Matt. 10:23.

Lystra. Who was healed through Paul's ministry at this town? Through what other apostles was an impotent man healed (3:1–6)? What did the people wish to do to Paul and Barnabas (14:13)? Which apostle had a somewhat similar experience (10:25, 26)? What talent of Paul is noted here (v. 12)? How lasting was their popularity (v. 19)?

Derbe. What did Paul do in this town (14:21)?

Lystra, Iconium and Antioch. What exhortation did Paul give to the disciples in these towns (v. 22)? What did he tell them to expect (v. 22)? What did he do before he left (v. 23)?

Pisidia. This is the province where Antioch was located.

Perga. What had happened here before (13:13)? What work was done in this town (14:25)?

Attalia. A seaport.

Antioch. Here the apostles reported their work.

Be able to name from memory the different places visited by Paul on his first journey, mentioning briefly what occurred at each place.

2. The council at Jerusalem. Chap. 15:1–35.

Chapter 15 records the convening of the first Christian council, called to settle a very important problem; namely, the relation of the Gentiles to the Jews and the grounds on which the former were to be saved. The two questions to be settled were: Are the Gentiles to keep the Law of Moses in order to be saved? And, are the Gentiles to have religious equality with the Jews?

> It must be remembered that the separation between Jew and Gentile was both religious and social. The Jews had a divine law which sanctioned the principle, and enforced the practice of national isolation. They could not easily believe that this law, with which all the glorious passages of their history was connected, was meant to endure only for a limited period; and we cannot but sympathize with the difficulty they felt in accepting the notion of a cordial union with the uncircumcised, even after idolatry was abandoned and morality observed. And again, the peculiar character of the religion which isolated the Jews was such as to place insuperable obstacles in the way of social union with other men. Their ceremonial observances precluded the possibility of their eating with the Gentiles. The nearest parallel we can find to this barrier between the Jew and Gentile is the institution of the caste among the populations of India, which presents itself to our politicians as a perplexing fact in the government of the presidencies, and to our missionaries as the great obstacle to Christianity in the East. A [Hindu] cannot eat with a [Parsi, a member of a Zoroastrian religious sect in India], or a [Muslim]—and among the [Hindus] themselves the meals of a Brahmin are polluted by the presence of a Pariah,—though they meet and have free [interaction] in the ordinary transaction of business. So it was in the patriarchal age. It was an abomination for the Egyptians to eat bread with the Hebrews. Gen. 43:32. The same principle was divinely sanctioned for a time in the Mosaic institutions. The Israelites who lived among the Gentiles, met them freely in their places of public resort,

buying and selling, conversing and disputing; but their families were separated. In the relations of domestic life, it was "unlawful," as Peter said to Cornelius, "for a man that was a Jew to keep company or come unto one of another nation." When Peter returned from the centurion at Caesarea to his brother Christians at Jerusalem, their great charge against him was that he had gone unto men uncircumcised and had eaten with them; and the weak compliance of which he was guilty, after the true principle of social unity had been publicly recognized, and which called forth the rebuke of his brother apostle, was that, after eating with the Gentiles, he 'withdrew and separated himself, fearing them which were of the circumcision.' Gal. 2:11, 12.

How these two difficulties, which seemed to forbid the formation of a united church, were ever to be overcome—how the Gentiles were to be religiously united without the enforced obligation of the whole Mosaic Law,—how they were to be socially united as equal brethren in the family of a common Father,—the solution in that day must have seemed impossible. And without the direct intervention of divine grace it would have been impossible. —Conybeare and Howson.

The question was made an issue by a certain party of Jewish believers, who, though acknowledging that God had granted eternal life unto the Gentiles, insisted that the observance of the Law of Moses was obligatory in their case, and that it was necessary to their salvation. The members of this party later became Paul's bitterest enemies, and at different periods of his ministry did all in their power to undermine his authority. Gal. 2:4. It was this class of men that caused the church of the Galatians to go back to the observance of the Mosaic law. Gal. 5:1–7. It should be remembered that these men, known as the Judaizers had the authority of Old Testament Scriptures to support their assertions. (The New Testament was not yet written.) The Old Testament predicted the salvation of the Gentiles (Ps. 22:7; 86:9; Isa. 49:6). But the Old Testament taught that the submitting to the rite of circumcision, and the observance of other Mosaic ceremonies was necessary for union with God's people. Gen. 17:14. So then there comes before us another aspect of the problem; namely, as to how the liberty of the Gospel and the authority of the Scriptures were to be preserved. This and the other problems find their solution in the speeches made by those present at the council.

Note Peter's discourse (15:7–11). His main argument is that the impartation of the Holy Ghost was the true test of God's acceptance of the Gentiles. The fact that the last-named received the gift of the Spirit as well as the Jews proves that God does not place any difference between Jewish and Gentile believers (v. 8). The fact that the Gentiles received the Spirit before submitting to any external ceremony shows that no outward observance of the Mosiac law was necessary to salvation. Though under the old covenant, circumcision was required as a condition for belonging to the chosen people, God's action in saving and baptizing the Gentiles without the observance of such a rite indicated that He had made a new covenant, and that the old was passing away. Jer. 31:31. It was by faith, not by the works of the law, that the Gentiles were justified (v. 9). God had delivered all believers from the heavy yoke of the Law; therefore to impose that burden on the Gentiles was tempting God (v. 10). The Jewish believers themselves were not saved by the law, but by grace (v. 11).

Paul and Barnabas contented themselves with telling what God had wrought among the Gentiles (v. 12). The fact that God was saving Gentiles, filling them with the Spirit and working miracles among them apart from any attempt on their part to keep the law, would prove that the latter was unnecessary to their salvation.

Peter had declared the equality of Jew and Gentile. But, the Pharisees might object, "How is this fact to be reconciled with the Scriptures that teach the supremacy of the Jews over the Gentiles?" Isa. 61:5, 6; Zech. 14:18. James anticipates this objection and answers it by outlining the divine program for the age. He first of all explains that not all the Gentiles will be saved during this age, but only certain individuals to make up, together with the Jewish elect, the Church (v. 14). Then will follow the restoration of Israel as a nation, and their consequent exaltation over nations (v. 16). After this, all the nations will turn to the Lord (v. 17).

Notice the decision of the council (vv. 19–29). The Gentiles were not required to be circumcised or keep the law of Moses. However, certain prohibitions were laid upon the Gentiles: they were to abstain from idolatry and fornication, and they were not to eat animals strangled, or the blood of those animals. Lev. 7:22–27. The first two prohibitions were dictated by the moral law; the other two, by the ceremonial. The sins of fornication and idolatry are mentioned because they are the two sins which would prove a special temptation to those saved from among the heathen. The last two prohibitions represented a concession to Jewish beliefs. However, there was no compromise in any fundamental matter.

> The most shameless violations of purity took place in connection with the sacrifices and feasts celebrated in honor of the heathen divinities. Everything, therefore, which tended to keep the Gentile converts even from accidental or apparent association with those scenes of vice, made their recovery from pollution more easy, and enabled the Jewish converts to look on their

new Christian brethren with less suspicion and antipathy. This seems to be the reason why we find an acknowledged sin mentioned in the decree along with ceremonial observances which were meant to be only temporary and perhaps local. We must look on the whole subject from the Jewish point of view, and consider how violations of morality and contradictions of the ceremonial law were associated together in the Gentile world. It is hardly necessary to remark that much additional emphasis is given to the moral part of the decree, when we remember that it was addressed to those who lived in proximity to the profligate sanctuaries of Antioch and Paphos. —Conybeare and Howson.

Notice the outcome of the council: it resulted in a victory for Paul's party and a recognition of his call and ministry. Gal. 2:9.

We shall conclude this subject by giving the four phases of that great truth—the union of Jew and Gentile in one body:

1. This truth was, in past ages, a **mystery**. Eph. 3:5, 6. The Old Testament taught the salvation of the Gentiles, but not their forming together with the Jews, one body.

2. It became a **revelation**. Acts 10:11–18, 34, 35; 15:7–9.

3. It became a **problem**. Acts Chap. 15.

4. It afterwards became a **reality**. Gal. 3:28.

CHAPTER XI

ACTS 15:36 TO 21:17

What unfortunate occurrence marked the beginning of the second missionary journey (15:36–39)? Did this hinder God's work at all? Was Barnabas or Mark ever mentioned again in the book of Acts? Who received the endorsement of the brethren (15:40)?

3. **Paul's second missionary journey. Chaps. 15:36 to 18:22.**

Let us now trace Paul's second journey (15:36 to 18:22). Following Dr. Hurlbut's arrangement we shall divide the journey into three sections: The stations in Asia, the stations in Europe, and the stations of the return.

Syria and **Cilicia**. In these two provinces Paul visited the churches that had already been established there.

Derbe. What happened the last time they were in this city (14:21)?

Lystra. Whom did Paul meet here? What was his nationality? What is said concerning his character?

Phrygia, **Galatia**, and **Mysia**. What limitation was placed upon Paul's ministry in these provinces? Why (16:9)?

Troas. What call did Paul receive here?

Philippi. Notice the humble beginning of the church in Europe—at a small prayer meeting. Then notice the first conflict of the apostles with heathendom (vv. 19–40). Here we find first mention of the fact of Paul's Roman citizenship (v. 37). This citizenship served him to good purpose later in his ministry. Those entitled to the privilege of Roman citizenship were those born in Rome (except slaves); those born in a Roman colony, i.e., a town to which was extended the rights of Roman citizenship (Philippi was such a town); those whose fathers were citizens (Paul may have obtained his citizenship this way); and those who purchased their citizenship. Acts 22:28. The following were the privileges of a Roman citizen: he could always claim protection by uttering the phrase, "I am a Roman citizen;" he could not be condemned without a trial; he could not be scourged; he could not be crucified; he could appeal from the common courts to the emperor.

Amphipolis, Apollonia. Paul did not stay very long in either of these towns.

Thessalonica. To whom did Paul preach first in this town? What was his message to them (17:3)? What two effects followed his preaching (vv. 4, 5)?

Berea. To whom did Paul preach first? What was the character of these Jews? What two effects followed the preaching of the Word (vv. 12, 13)? Who remained in Berea while Paul left for Athens?

Athens. Notice Paul's encounter with members of two schools of philosophy—the Epicureans and the Stoics. (Philosophy is that branch of knowledge which has for its object the discovery of the truth concerning God, man, and the universe, as far as those truths can be ascertained by the human reason.) The Epicureans were skeptics who rejected all religion. They believed that the world rose from chance, that the soul is mortal, and that pleasure is the ultimate end of life. The Stoics were pantheists; i.e., they believed that everything is part of God. They believed that virtue is the chief end of life, and should be practiced for its sake alone. Notice Paul's message. He shows God's relation to the universe (vv. 24, 25) and to man (vv. 26–29). He then declares God's moral government of the world, this government to be perfectly manifest at the last judgment (v. 31). What were the two effects of the preaching (vv. 32–34)?

Corinth. Whom did Paul meet at this city? Who joined Paul here? What was the effect of his preaching to the Jews? What encouragement did Paul have to remain in spite of opposition (18:9)? How long did Paul remain at Corinth? Who protected Paul at this time (v. 12)?

It was from Corinth that Paul wrote his two epistles to the Thessalonians. These were written for the purpose of confirming the young converts, comforting them in the face of persecution, exhorting them to holiness, and comforting them concerning their dead.

Cenchrea. This was a seaport near Corinth from which Paul sailed. Had a church been established here? Rom. 16:1.

Ephesus. Whom did Paul leave here (18:19)? What ministry did Priscilla and Aquila have there later (18:26)? Why was he in a hurry to return to Jerusalem (v. 21)? What did he promise to do before he left (v. 21)?

Cæsarea. This was the Roman capital of Palestine, and a harbor.

Jerusalem. Paul stopped here to salute the church (18:22).

Antioch. Here he reported the results of his missionary journey.

4. Paul's third missionary journey. Chaps. 18:23 to 21:17.

Antioch. The starting point of all Paul's missionary journeys.

Galatia and Phrygia. Paul traveled through these provinces confirming and encouraging the believers of the churches he had established there.

Ephesus. Notice the preparation for Paul's three years' ministry in this town (18:24). Apollos, a cultured Alexandrian Jew, had been preaching John the Baptist's message, thus paving the way for Paul's fuller revelation of Christ and His salvation. What was Paul's earnest desire for all believers (19:2)? What did he later write to the believers of this city? Eph. 5:18. Were these men really saved before receiving the Spirit (19:5; compare 8:36, 37)? What happened after they were saved (v. 6)? How long did Paul preach in the synagogue? What did he do when opposition arose? How long did he continue preaching in the school of Tyrannus (v. 10)? How far did the Word of God spread from Ephesus (v. 10)?

Notice that **special** miracles were wrought by Paul at Ephesus. This was granted Paul, because Ephesus was the headquarters of idolatry in Asia. It was a stronghold of the powers of darkness. Because of this God gave additional power to His servant to triumph over Satan. Some professional exorcists (those who made a business of casting out demons) attempted to use that name through which Paul had performed miracles. They suffered severely for their rashness. Their punishment taught the Ephesians that the name of Jesus was a powerful name, a sacred name which could not be taken in vain (19:17). Many believers were affected by this incident and confessed some of their sins, especially the sin of dabbling in the occult sciences (vv. 18, 19). Then followed a great revival (v. 20). Notice that Paul's missionary vision is widening; he must preach at Rome (v. 21). Verses 23 to 41 record an incident which testifies in a concrete way of Paul's success in Ephesus. He had struck such a blow at this great fortress of Satan that the worship of Diana was waning. This alarmed the makers of idols who raised an uproar against Paul.

During his stay at Ephesus, Paul wrote the first epistle to the Corinthians. After Paul's departure, serious disorders broke out in the Corinthian church. The church was divided; immorality was tolerated, brother was suing brother at law, and the Lord's Supper had been degraded to the level of a common meal, where drunkenness was common. To correct these abuses, and to answer some questions they had asked concerning marriage, meat and the gifts of the Spirit, Paul wrote them a letter.

Macedonia (20:2). It is probable that Paul visited Philippi, Thessalonica and Berea at this time. It was here that Paul wrote his second letter to the Corinthians. It was written to encourage the great body of the church which had repented on receiving his first letter, and to warn a small party that persisted in despising his commands.

Greece (20:2). Paul's chief mission in this country was to visit the church of Corinth to correct abuses, and to deal with a rebellious minority that refused to acknowledge his authority. While at Corinth he wrote the epistles to the Galatians and the Romans. The former was written to restore the church of the Galatians which, influenced by legalistic preachers, had begun to observe the law of Moses as a means of salvation and sanctification. The second was written to give the Roman church a statement of the great truths which Paul preached and to make known his intention of visiting them.

Philippi. Leaving Greece, Paul set out for Jerusalem (19:21). Paul's party went ahead of him to Troas (20:4, 5).

Troas. How long did Paul remain here? On what day was it customary for the church to gather for its weekly services (20:7)? Is there any other scripture that bears this out? 1 Cor. 16:1, 2. What incident occurred here?

Assos. While the rest of the party sailed from Troas, Paul went on foot to this town, where he was picked up by the ship.

Mitylene, Chios, Samos. Small islands where Paul's ship touched.

Trogyllium. A town on the coast of Asia Minor

Miletus. While the ship was delayed here, Paul called the elders of the Ephesian church and gave them a farewell address. In verses 17 to 21 Paul reviews his ministry among them. How had he served the Lord (v. 19)? How thorough was his ministry (v. 20)? What was his message (v. 21)? What was facing him (vv. 22, 23)? What were his feelings in the face of this (v. 24)? Had Paul fulfilled his responsibility among them (v. 26)? How (v. 27, compare Ezek. 33:1–9)? What admonition does he give to the elders (v. 28)? What warning does he give in view of what coming dangers (v. 29)? Had Paul merely **preached** the Gospel among them (v. 35)?

Coos, Rhodes. Two small islands off the coast of Asia Minor.

Patara. Here the apostle changed ships.

Tyre. What message did Paul receive here? 21:4.

Ptolemais. How long did Paul remain here?

Cæsarea. Here Paul's coming persecutions in Jerusalem were prophesied. Before answering in the negative the question as to whether Paul was in the Lord's will in going to Jerusalem, the following fact should be noted: Paul was ever obedient to the Lord's leading (16:6–10); his words in 21:13 are those of a person who feels he is then in God's will; others saw in Paul's attitude God's will (21:14); it was not natural for a man like Paul to expose himself needlessly to danger; the things that he suffered in Jerusalem were not necessarily a sign that he was out of God's will (Acts 9:16; 23:11); it was the Lord's will that Paul appear before Nero (27:24). It may be possible that the disciples of Tyre (21:4) predicted through the Spirit Paul's coming persecution, and then added their own advice.

Jerusalem. As soon as Paul arrived in this city, the church council gathered to hear Paul's report.

CHAPTER XII

ACTS 21:18 TO 28:31

IV. The Closing Scenes of Paul's life.

Chaps. 21:18 to 28:31.

1. Paul and the Jewish Christians. 21:18–26.
2. Paul and the non-Christian Jews. 21:27–31.
3. Paul's arrest. 21:32–40.
4. Paul's defense before the Jews and the result. 22:1–30.
5. Paul before the Jewish council. 23:1–10.
6. His removal to Caesarea. 23:11–35.
7. Paul before Felix. Chap. 24.
8. Paul before Festus. Chap. 25.
9. Paul before Agrippa. Chap. 26.
10. Paul's journey to Rome. Chaps. 27, 28.

Paul was well received by the church at Jerusalem (21:17, 18), but they felt anxious for his safety, for the rumor had spread that Paul was preaching against the law of Moses and that he was persuading the Jews to forsake it. Because of this rumor (which was false) the Jews of Jerusalem felt toward Paul as we would feel toward an anarchist—one opposed to law and order. In order to disarm the Jews' hostility, and to prove the falsity of the rumor, Paul consented to the observance of a Jewish ceremony. In doing this, he did not compromise in any fundamental matter, but acted upon the following principles laid down by himself in his writings: he became a Jew to the Jews that he might win the Jews, as willingly as he became as a Gentile in order to win the Gentiles (1 Cor. 9:20, 21); he had given it as a rule that no man should change his external observances because he became a Christian. 1 Cor. 7:17–19. Paul's action in regard to testimony to Timothy (16:3) proved the falsity of the accusation that he was persuading the Jews to forsake the law of Moses. In advising Paul to perform a ceremony of the Jewish ritual, James assured him that no compromise in the matter of the grounds of Gentile salvation was implied (v. 25).

Paul's action did not save him from the enmity of the non-Christian Jews (vv. 27–31). Certain ones who had heard him preach in Asia Minor (v. 27), recognized him and immediately stirred up the population against him. But for the intervention of the Roman soldiers Paul would have been killed.

Notice Paul's defense (22:1–21). He assured them that his present beliefs and life could not be the result of an original difference between himself and his hearers, for he was a true Jew (v. 3), taught by the greatest Jewish teacher of the day (v. 3), and he was just as zealous for the law, and opposed to the Christians as they were (vv. 4, 5). Paul then showed what caused his change of belief, and his attitude toward the Christians; namely, a vision of the Lord himself (vv. 6–16). The reason why he was preaching to the despised Gentiles was that the Lord himself had sent him (vv. 17–21). Notice what happened at the mention of the Gentiles (v. 22).

Notice how Paul's Roman citizenship protected him at this time (22:25). The words "I am a Roman citizen," uttered in any part of the empire were sufficient to bring protection to the one speaking them.

Paul was then brought before the Jewish council, and there he declared his innocence (23:1). The unjust and cruel action of the high priest in commanding him to be smitten, caused him to break forth into a severe denunciation against him. In the heat of his indignation he forgot the high priest and saw only a tyrannical ruler. Though he could not honor the man, he honored the office he occupied (v. 5). It is interesting to note that Paul's denunciation of the high priest was prophetical, for some twelve years later, the latter died a violent death.

Seeing that the council was prejudiced against him, and there was no hope of justice and mercy from them, Paul resorted to a stratagem. He knew that the Pharisees and Sadducees were divided on the doctrine of the resurrection. Therefore he appealed to the Pharisaic section of the council, and appealed for their clemency on the ground that he was on trial because of the preaching of a doctrine which they themselves accepted. This appeal divided the council, and led to Paul's escape and his protection by the Romans. Later, the discovery of a plot to assassinate Paul led to his being escorted to Caesarea by a company of Roman soldiers. At this town he appeared before the governor, Felix.

We shall notice here the accusations brought against Paul and his answers to them (24:1–21). In this discourse and the one made before Agrippa we shall follow the analysis given by Dr. Stifler.

The accusation was three-fold (vv. 5, 6); sedition, "a mover of sedition among the Jews"; heresy, "a ringleader of the sect of the Nazarenes"; sacrilege— "who also hath gone about to profane the temple." He disproved the accusation of sedition by showing the time was too short (v. 11), that his conduct disproved it (v. 12), and that there was no proof of it (v. 13). In answer to the charge of heresy, he affirmed his belief in the Jewish Scriptures (v. 14), and professed to having the same hope as the Jews themselves (vv. 15, 16). That he had not committed sacrilege was evident, for he had brought alms and offerings to his nation (v. 17), he was found in the temple purified (v. 18), and there were no witnesses present to prove the charge (v. 19).

Notice Felix's attitude toward Paul in public (vv. 22, 23), in private (v. 25), and the outcome of the trial (v. 27).

Paul was then brought before Festus, the new governor (25:1). Seeing that Festus was friendly toward the Jews (25:9), he availed himself of his right as a Roman citizen to appeal to the emperor (v. 11). This took the case completely out of the hands of Festus.

Notice Paul's defense before Agrippa (Chap. 26). It is an argument to justify his belief and preaching of the resurrection. This belief, Paul affirms is no crime, for Paul has always been a Pharisee whose prime article of faith has been the same hope (vv. 4–6). His accusers believe this same doctrine and are inconsistent in attacking him (v. 7). Paul did not come of himself to the preaching of the Gospel, for he was formerly opposed to it (vv. 8–12). It was a revelation of Jesus that brought him into the ministry (vv. 13–18). It was an obedience to this divine revelation that was the only cause of the Jewish opposition (vv. 19–22). His teaching concerning Christ's death and resurrection agrees with the teaching of Moses and the prophets (vv. 22, 23).

What was the effect of this discourse on Felix? On Agrippa?

We shall now trace Paul's journey to Rome (Chaps. 27, 28).

Cæsarea. From this port, where he had been a prisoner two years, Paul sailed to Rome. As companions he had Aristarchus (27:2) and Luke (indicated by the use of the pronoun "we").

Sidon. Here Paul was allowed to visit his friends.

Myra. A city on the south coast of Asia Minor, where Paul changed ships.

Cnidus. A port on the coast of Asia Minor. The vessel was unable to enter because of contrary winds.

Crete. An island south of Greece.

Fair Havens. Here the ship remained for some time. Paul's advice was that they should remain in this harbor during the winter, and so escape a danger which he foresaw. The master of the ship did not accept this advice, but attempted to reach the port of Phenice. Their attempt was thwarted by a storm which arose. Paul's prediction was fulfilled. For fourteen days and nights they were driven about until they came to the island of Melita.

Melita. How long did Paul remain in this island (28:11)?

Syracuse. A town on the eastern shore of the island of Sicily. The ship remained here three days.

Rhegium. A town at the extreme end of the Italian mainland.

Puteoli. One of the leading ports of Italy. Here Paul found some brethren.

Appii Forum, the "Three Taverns." Two villages where the Roman brethren came to meet Paul.

Rome. The first thing that Paul did after arriving at Rome was to call the Jewish leaders in order that he might clear himself from the charge against him, and to obtain a friendly hearing. It was his last recorded attempt to win the Jews. Notice the result of his preaching to them (28:24–28; compare Matt. 13:13–15; John 12:40; Matt. 21:43).

Dr. Griffith-Thomas notices God's providence in Paul's imprisonment in the following way:

1. He was safe from all the Jews.

2. He became conspicuous to all. Phil. 1:12, 13.

3. He had an opportunity of witnessing to the soldiers who guarded him.

4. He was visited by friends from various churches. (Phil. 2:25; 4:10).

5. He was able to write some of his choicest epistles: Philippians, Philemon, Colossians, Ephesians.

From tradition and some references, it has been concluded that Paul was released for about a period of two years (see Phil. 1:24–26; 2:24; Philemon 24:2 Tim. 4:17), and then was rearrested and finally executed during the persecution of the Christians by Nero. During this period of liberty it is believed that he wrote the epistles to Timothy and to Titus.

Because of its importance we have covered the book of Acts somewhat more thoroughly than the preceding books. We shall now ask the student to learn the following chapter outline in order to impress upon his mind the contents of the book:

CHAPTER

1. Power.
2. Pentecost.
3. Peter and John.
4. Priests and prayer.
5. Punishment.
6. Poor Christians.
7. Persecuted Stephen.
8. Philip.
9. Paul's conversion.
10. Peter's vision.
11. Peter's explanation.
12. Peter's imprisonment.
13. Paul's first missionary journey.
14. Paul's return.
15. Paul at Jerusalem.
16. Paul's second journey.
17. Paul at Athens.
18. Priscilla and Aquila.
19. Paul's third journey.
20. Paul in Europe.
21. Paul's arrest.
22. Paul's staircase address.
23. Paul's escape.
24. Paul before Felix.
25. Paul before Festus.
26. Paul before Agrippa.
27. Paul shipwrecked.
28. Paul at Rome.

NOTES